What People Are Saying
About This

"Mark is an important voice in the landscape of life, and this is a book that every individual - male or female - should read."

> TAMMY KLING, Founder – The Conversation. Author of *Words*

"The ego driven life is conventional. We all start there. Over time we have great challenges that invite us to examine the questions of identity and destiny. When we examine those questions everything changes. This is a book that gives witness to the journey and insight to the traveler. It is a book we would all do well to read."

> ROBERT E. QUINN, Center for Positive Organizations, University of Michigan, Author of *The Economics of Higher Purpose*

"Self-awareness is the meta-skill of the 21st Century. The journey to greater self-insight requires courage and intentionality. In Mark's compelling work, you will be inspired and challenged to examine your own narrative, your blind spots and how you want to show up."

> DR. TASHA EURICH, *New York Times* best-selling author of *Insight and Bankable Leadership*

Your guide to get from the prison of self-focused narcissism to the freedom of skillful love and vulnerability has arrived. Mark Freier can guide you because he has walked the path himself. As a friend and professional colleague, I have had a front row seat. Mark has that unique ability to master a theory by working it out through his own relationships. In short, Mark is the real deal. In this book he articulates both the vision and practical plan to get the job done. You will not only enjoy this book, but you will also walk away with what you need to transform your own life. I recommend this book wholeheartedly!

Dr. Tim Hogan, PsyD, LP, CIRT, Certified Imago Relationship Therapist, Co-author, *How to Find the Help You Need*, a guide to spiritual direction and psychotherapy

"Change is never easy. Mark's personal journey of transformation is about choices toward a more positive mindset. As you read his griping story you will see how one person's transformation sends ripples of positivity and hope through his relationships. His true colors shine through in both the good and challenging times."

Shawn Achor, *New York Times* best-selling Author of *The Happiness Advantage* and *Big Potential*

THE CHOICE TO

SHOW UP

Who I Am Matters

THE CHOICE TO

SHOW UP

Who I Am Matters

Mark R. Freier

Join the conversation at
www.thechoicetoshowup.com

Clovercroft Publishing

The Choice to Show Up

©2020 by Mark Freier

Published by Clovercroft Publishing, Franklin, Tennessee

Edited by OnFire Books

Copy Edit by Lee Titus Elliott

Cover Design by Debbie Manning Sheppard

Interior Design by Suzanne Lawing

Printed in the United States of America

978-1-950892-20-4

DEDICATION

For my best friend and love of my life, Debbie. She tells me she married me for an adventure. While she wouldn't have scripted this one, she faithfully, unconditionally, and passionately has taught me for over forty years to authentically make the choice to show up. She is my inspiration, my role model—my hero of how to live life fully in the present moment as a transformational person. I am forever grateful.

A whole new world
A dazzling place I never knew
But when I'm way up here
It's crystal clear
That now I'm in a whole new world with you

Aladdin and Princess Jasmine
(A Whole New World—Lea Salonga, Brad Kane)

Preface

Decades ago, my wife urged me to purchase a pin from Disney World. "You should really buy this pin. It symbolizes an important truth!" she exhorted. When she handed it to me, I understood the reason; it was a pin of Goofy dressed up as Mickey Mouse.

In case you need a refresher, Goofy is the tall, anthropomorphic dog with a Southern drawl, who typically wears a turtle neck and vest, with pants, shoes, white gloves, and a tall hat originally designed as a rumpled fedora. Goofy is a close friend of Mickey Mouse and Donald Duck and is one of Disney's most recognizable characters. He is normally characterized as clumsy and dimwitted, yet there are times when Goofy is shown as intuitive, and clever. We like Goofy. Whether it's hearing him say "gawrsh!" laughing with "ah-hyuck!" or watching him be a bit eccentric, he is fun-loving and makes us smile.

My pin is distinctively unique in that Goofy is wearing Mickey's iconic red shorts, large yellow shoes, white gloves, and he is sporting Mickey's ears. With a wry smile and a half-hearted wave, the Goofy in my pin looks completely out of character and uncomfortable in his own skin.

My wife wanted me to have this pin as a reminder that I need to be myself. Acting out or posing as someone else isn't becoming, nor is it authentic. She strongly urged me to write about this Goofy pin. It sits in a prominent place in my home office. I look at it every time I sit at my desk. It's more than symbolic for me. It's a reminder that I am best when I am just myself.

.

Contents

Acknowledgements 13

Introduction   17

Chapter 1   Stories Matter 23

Chapter 2   Uncovering Story Themes 31

Chapter 3   What's Really Happening Inside 41

Chapter 4   The Fall of a Kingdom 53

Chapter 5   Good 'Ole Country Western Blues Song . . . 59

Chapter 6   From Transmitting to Transforming 67

Chapter 7   Finding Your Sweet Spot 79

Chapter 8   Living Out of Mission 89

Chapter 9   Accepting Help 95

Chapter 10   Open to Surprises 101

Chapter 11   Learning the Gift of Gratitude 105

Chapter 12   Morphing Dynamics 115

Chapter 13   The "No Conflict" Rule 121

Chapter 14   Community Is Messy 129

Chapter 15   Present-Moment Living 141

Chapter 16   The Benefit of Experience
(Mentoring and Coaching) 149

Chapter 17   The Positive Choice 155

Chapter 18   Who's Watching the Margin 163

Chapter 19   Being a Friend........................169

Chapter 20   My Resolve..........................179

Appendix 1   Letter to a College Student 183

Appendix 2   Ten Things I Learned about
                  Transformation......................187

About the Author....................................189

Join the conversation at
www.thechoicetoshowup.com

Acknowledgements

Whenever I share my story, I am frequently asked when I will write a book. I routinely shrug it off and make excuses that no one would read it. I enjoy books by others and often muse whether I had a book "in me." To all those who have asked, urged, and inspired me to write, I am grateful that you, knowingly or unknowingly, poured into my life and sparked something in me to write this book.

A special thank-you to my wife, Deb. I've dedicated the book to you. I've talked about how I admire you. And it's worth saying that I am beyond words in expressing my gratitude for your love and powerful, positive presence in my life.

My kids have lived through my transformational journey. While they grew up in our family, they have their own unique and powerful stories. In the past, I have overshared stories about them. I have learned my lesson. Their stories are theirs to tell. Today, they live full, passionate lives, with beautiful, serving hearts. Thank you, Anne, Katie (Dan), and Nathan (Angela). I love you and treasure my moments with you!

To my grandchildren: Abigail, Graham, and Logan. You bring so much joy to "Papa." Thank you.

To all the individuals I have had the opportunity to lead, to be led by, or to watch their leadership up close and from afar, you have laid the foundation for this book.

There are so many people who have impacted my life.

Many are mentioned in this book. I want to express my special thanks to

- Tim Hogan, for being such a great friend, for hours of rich discussions at Starbucks, for believing in me, for reading the first draft, and for strongly urging me to get this book published. I trust you.

- Matt Emhoff, I am grateful that you go after what you want and that part of what you go after is time with me. Our conversations are special. By the way, thanks for giving a couple of chapters of the first draft to Patrick Davidson and Dan Bumford (believing I would agree with you) so that I could hear their reactions and the words, "I can't wait to read the rest of the book."

- Patrick Davidson, you are a true friend at every level. You love me, you challenge me, you encourage me, you allow me to push into your life with the same tenacity you push into my life. While the Irish whiskey or bourbon and cigars we share are good, they pale to the depth of our conversations and the admiration I have for you. Here's to many more years of shared tears, belly laughs, and stories about leadership and life.

- The other men of True Pursuit: Dan Bumford, Pete Emhoff, Brad Jones, Ross Martin, and our long-distance member, Jeff Emhoff, as we enjoy and wrestle with all that makes up authentic community.

OnFire Books lives by the mantra, "We use words to change lives!" From the time Tammy Kling and Tiarra Thompkins first read this manuscript and throughout the process of reading it, they have graciously and freely offered more encouragement and support than one could imagine. I am so grateful for your expertise, and I admire your commitment to changing the world and to believing in me and my story.

I want to recognize the valuable help of Larry Carpenter and Clovercroft Publishing. Your guidance for newbies like me blaze the way for making publishing a reality.

A sincere thank you to my proofreaders Dan Bumford, Patrick Davidson and Ashley O'Neil. You added so much value by asking me to clarify or rethink experiences and premises to make more sense.

Chris Elias, thank you for being a leader I trust and respect. Thank you for being a partner with me in Nexecute. You make me and everything we do better.

Writing a book at this season of my life means that I have decades of people who have crossed my path. Albeit for short seasons, each has an important part in contributing to who I am. To be honest, some will not have fond memories of me. If you're one of those people reading this, I hope you can extend me grace and read on. On the other hand, if you have good memoires of working with me, listening to my messages, or participating in my training, thank you. This gives you a glimpse into my journey and how grateful I am today. Please know that transformation is a choice, and I made it!

And, lastly, to you, the reader. Thank you for reading my story. I hope that, in reading it, you will embrace the sacredness of your story; the tenacity by which you persevere through challenges and how to show up. I hope you approach your story with gleeful curiosity and grace. Your story matters!

There comes a point in your life when you need to stop reading other people's books and write your own. – ALBERT EINSTEIN

Introduction

What do you know about transformational people? True confession: I didn't know much about them.

Growing up and into my early adult life, I figured that everyone was on life's journey. Sure, there were different types of people from different backgrounds, race, religion, and socioeconomic status, but that was about it. There were those who "made it" and those who didn't. My definition of those who "made it" meant levels of material success measured in the cars they drove and their proximity to where they lived near Lake Michigan. I grew up in southwest Michigan, and the closer you lived to the big lake or any other inland lake was a clear measure of success.

> AN OUTWARD MEASURE OF SUCCESS IN NO WAY INDICATES HOW PEOPLE EXPERIENCE YOU; THAT IS, HOW YOU "SHOW UP" TO THE WORLD.

What I didn't realize is that an outward measure of success in no way indicates how people experience you; that is, how you "show up" to the world. You can be outwardly successful and show up as arrogant, self-centered, condescending, and so forth. You can also have little measure of outward success and show up as self-righteous, judgmental, rude, and so on. Maybe, just maybe, there was something more than what could be seen.

For a boy who grew with a generational family motto, *What will people think?* which I believe was some form of curse—that seemed odd. I was taught life was about presenting a good front and appearing to have it all together. What mattered was what people achieved and how self-disciplined they were. At its worst, my opinions and passions were not valued. At its best, my success was measured by whether or not people liked me. I learned how to be duplicitous, how to pose, and how get from people what I wanted. It was a transactional life. For me it was empty. Have you ever just been an actor in your own story?

What happens to a person who cultivates that type of mind-set? I was floored when I was confronted by Robert Quinn's statement in *Change the World*, "In transactional systems, people put themselves first...others are not inherently valued...only by what they contribute to the exchange. People become objects." No wonder a staff person once blurted, "You know, you are really good on stage, but, truth is, during the week you are an asshole!" Obviously, my transactional life wasn't working.

This book is about being a transformational person. Even more profoundly for me, it's about leadership—being a person of influence. Because transformational people become transformational leaders.

Transformational leaders distinguish themselves from transactional leaders in that life and business is not just about

THE FUNDAMENTAL CHARACTERISTIC OF TRANSFORMATIONAL LEADERS IS SELF-AWARENESS, FOLLOWED BY A DESIRE FOR SELF-MANAGEMENT. quid pro quo or just providing a service for which they are reimbursed. It's not about getting from people what you want or focusing on WHAT you do. Rather, beliefs and behaviors first flow from WHO they are: authentic, honest, and humble. When you are around them, there is a strong sense of connection and energy of service.

Transformational leaders are committed to two fundamental principles. The first is personal development. The fundamental characteristic of transformational leaders is self-awareness, followed by the action step of self-management. They know that real change happens from the inside-out. Therefore, they ruthlessly choose to pay attention to their interior world and know that, by doing so, it will impact their exterior world. The second characteristic is about how they approach work. They embrace change: they accept change, identify what needs to change, create a vision for change, and inspire change throughout the organization, thereby attracting people to sacrifice perceived self-interest for a genuinely appealing collective purpose.

It all starts with answering the question Rafiki asked Simba in *The Lion King,* "Who are you?"

Answering this question has been a life-long quest. Not knowing the answer has led to decades of confusion, blindly reacting instead of proactively identifying the results I want to create, striving for the wrong validation, and making destructive decisions. These are not the lost years; rather, they are the discovery years that have led me to clarify WHO I am today.

- I am broken. This means I can embrace my vulnerabilities and admit that I am weak. I don't have to have all the answers, create an image, be perceived as right or perfect, or long to have people like me.

- I am beloved. I am loved by God. I have inherent worth, and, therefore, I am enough. I can fully be myself and embrace my strengths and weaknesses, my flaws and imperfections. I can bring my best self to others and to the world. I can bring joy.

Because I am broken and beloved, I can authentically live out my uniqueness:

- I love to capture beauty all around me; noticing and celebrating it.

- I love to innovate and blaze new trails of thought and practice.

- I love to inspire a new reality; bringing my passion.

- I am a husband, father, and grandfather—"Papa." I am a friend, a business partner, and a trusted advisor.

I am glad you picked up this book. I am living testimony to the power of inner transformation. My story has shaped my beliefs and practices that have changed my world and have impacted the lives of others with whom I come in contact.

Specifically, about this book:

I know what it means to make decisions that are based upon EGO and self-protection. I know what it means to try to get from other people what they cannot give you: validation. I know the impact of spending a lifetime of motivating people to see things my way and not having the insight to know that they saw through me and the selfishness of my motivations. I know what it's like to be so wounded and not have the courage to face it, and, by not facing it, inflicting my woundedness on others, mostly subconsciously. I know what it means to have to come to "the end of my rope" and know that the only healthy choice was to surrender and learn to change from the inside out.

I KNOW WHAT IT'S LIKE TO BE SO WOUNDED AND NOT HAVE THE COURAGE TO FACE IT, AND, BY NOT FACING IT, INFLICTING MY WOUNDEDNESS ON OTHERS, MOSTLY SUBCONSCIOUSLY.

I also know what it's like to live honestly, authentically, and with inner freedom. I know what it means to serve others out of settled purpose and clear values. I know what it means to be transformative.

I know what it's like to show up...as me! It is time for you to learn how to find that power inside of you so you can show up every day as the authentic you. Are you ready?

There is no greater agony than bearing an untold story inside you. –Maya Angelou

It's time to read your own life, because your story is the one that could set us all ablaze. –Dan B. Allender

CHAPTER 1

Stories Matter

I love stories. When I listen to stories, whether in person, by podcast, or by video, I am flooded with the gambit of emotions. There are probably a few reasons, but the one that tops the list is that I believe every person has a story and every story matters. I have learned from Dr. Brené Brown that stories tell us WHO we are, WHERE we come from, and WHAT we are up against. Hang around me long enough, and you will hear my say, "Tell me your story!"

It hasn't always been like that. For a good part of my life, I didn't like to hear other peoples' stories, nor did I care to. I would look at their lives, where they worked and lived, and how they spent their free time, and then I'd write their story for them. Good or bad, I wrote it, and it stayed until they proved otherwise. Of course, I never told them the story I wrote about them. It was a menagerie in my head. It didn't matter if there were snippets of truth. I was the author of what I wanted to believe about them. And while it may appear that I cared about their lives—I had become adept at using the narratives I wrote to make me seem empathic and interested—there was way too much of me that used perceived caring to my end. Sounds horribly arrogant. It was.

The Key to Unlock Our Story

Why would a young boy from a small Midwestern town that bordered Lake Michigan and raised in a parochial home think this way? That question has been answered by my therapist, my wife, and my two good friends—a Ph.D. in Human Behavior and a Psy.D. While I know our friendship is rooted in a deep mutual respect and love, I often joked that I was as much a case study for them as a friend. The truth is I have learned the motivations exuding from hubris, that my story matters and that, hidden in my story, are keys that unlock some of the ways in which my unique personality interpreted life and then learned how to cope.

My parents loved me. They provided for me. They did the best they could. And, like all other parents, out of their woundedness, they provided wounds for me. It isn't the parents' intent to wound children. It just happens. It's part of life. And when parents have unhealed pain, they transmit that pain to their children.

The challenge we face is what do we do with those wounds. How do we interpret them? What becomes the go-to messages of our inner critic? What vows or agreements do we make to survive and show up to the world?

I grew up a pastor's kid. For those of you who are pastors' kids, missionaries' kids, professors' kids or for those of you who know them well, you understand that when you mix in the God component, as well as living in the public eye, there are layers of stuff to unpack. The stuff messes with your mind and toys with your emotions. I know this is true for me and for many kids like me, who had to deal with the same stuff. In fact, when I share some of my struggles, almost every time, one of those kids, now an adult, comes up to me and whispers through tears, "I thought I was the only one." None of us want to blame our parents. Yet there is a secret suffering that comes when parents pledge to serve in public ministry. It's not talked about, because to do so would seem to dishonor the parents. The path to healing is gut-wrenching and soul-searching. It is loaded with shame. For those who choose to dig into the depths of this pain, there is redemption. However, let me be clear. The redemption is a personal redemption and often does not include a redemption with the family where the pain originated.

If you are one of those kids, I understand some of your journey and identify with your pain. If you know one of these kids, listen to their story. Don't try to fix them; just listen, empathize, and cry with them. Love them to hope and healing.

The Impact of Our Story

Let's get real. How do you interpret your wounds? What is the go-to message of your inner critic? What vows or agreements have you made?

One way you might find answers to those questions is to assess your style of relating. This would be the "go-to" way you relate when you feel vulnerable. "Vulnerable" comes from the Latin word meaning "to wound." Therefore, when vulnerable, we habitually show up in one of the three categories introduced by neopsychoanalytic theorist, Dr. Karen Horney. She proposed that children develop predictable ways of coping along three dimensions that show up in adulthood: a child can *move toward* people (compliance), *move against* them (domination), or *move away* from them (withdrawal).

My sister is a *move toward*. Even though we are only a few years apart, she is as compliant as they come. She is a peacekeeper. Not to be confused with a peacemaker. A peacemaker recognizes that they need to approach conflict head-on and with grace. I was neither of these. While we lived in the same home, my approach to life was to *move against*. Rules were meant to be tested, pushed, and broken, if necessary, to prove a point. I acted out aggressively or passive-aggressively, whatever I needed to do to get attention at any given moment. My sister behaved passively. I was regularly spanked. She was consistently coddled. In fact, she would often ask me, "Can't you just keep your mouth shut so you don't get another spanking?" "Nope!" At some morbid level, spankings were badges of courage. I got the attention I wanted…and survived. Any attention was worth it.

I found myself longing for attention, specifically from my female teachers. Fortunately, when I entered elementary school, I received it. My female teachers were kind, caring, and understanding. They seemed to smile when I was around them. They mirrored delight. It was as if their faces lit up when they saw me. Their actions toward me offered some type of emotional grounding. However, that ended abruptly in third grade. As I write, I do so with a level of chagrin. My third-grade teacher, who happened to be a female, was the exact opposite of every teacher I had before. On her best days, she was stern, uncompromising, and demanding. As a young boy who wanted to be liked, her behavior was devastating. There were no smiles. There was no understanding, and, in its place, was disdain. My talking, my very personality seemed to annoy her. I clearly remember being banned from most recesses, being put "in the corner," and, most of all, writing sentences, hundreds and hundreds of sentences. Remember that this was third grade.

One day, as she was playing the "Star-Spangled Banner" on the piano with her back to the class, a girl in my class said, "Freier, you're so ugly you make me laugh!" The whole class erupted in laughter. My teacher turned around and, without asking a question, blurted, "All of you are assigned 500 sentences. I want you all to go home and tell your parents it's Mark Freier's fault." Sullenly, I walked into my house. When my dad asked how many sentences I had to write, he just accepted that this was the deal for me, I told him the story. How the girl had made fun of me and how the teacher had blamed me. He immediately walked to the school (remember, my dad was the pastor and superintendent of the school). My teacher confirmed her story. One that put me at fault. My dad came home and spanked me for lying to him and not respecting my teacher. He reminded me how others are impacted by my misbehavior and grounded me to my room…for days.

Subconsciously, a deeper resentment was birthed in me. Women were supposed to be nurturing, safe, and understanding. That day proved my premise to be false. It would take me years, meeting my wife, and, decades later, in intense counseling from a strong, gracious woman, to see the devastation of that burgeoning resentment and how it shaped my view of women and ultimately how I treated women. I learned to show up with women with a passive-aggressive attitude and behaviors all meant to protect me. While I wouldn't recognize this for a long time, subconsciously I vowed I would never let a woman do that to me again. If I couldn't get some validation from women, I would ignore them. Fast forward to my days at an all-male college and seminary and it's easy to see how that vow was reinforced. Ignoring women is pretty easy when you have little interactions with them. See how subconscious vows matter?

The rest of my elementary years were okay. I buckled down. For the most part, I got good grades. Except in fourth grade when I got a C in religion. Pastor's kids don't get a C in religion. Whoops! I got attention all right.

> THE THIRST FOR BEING BETTER IS RARELY SATISFIED. COMPARISON IS THE GAME, AND WINNING IS OFTEN SUBJECTIVE.

Kids who have to *move against the grain* grow up to be adults who need to be correct, who need to win, and who are focused on being good. They work hard—in fact, harder than most people, because achievement is the reward. Performance—great performance—is expected, and feelings are discounted. Ambition wins over real love. Decades of that type of living strokes the EGO and is the seedbed for narcissism. The thirst for being better is rarely satisfied. Comparison is the game, and winning is often subjective.

My dad introduced me to Mr. Nye, southwestern Michigan's largest apple farmer, at age eleven. The introduction involved a wide-eyed kid ogling over large farm equipment and exploring the massive refrigeration units. At the end of this adventure, my dad simply said, "You're going to work for Mr. Nye this summer. You start tomorrow." I couldn't believe my ears. Sure, I was getting paid, $1.10 per hour, but I lost my freedom that summer. And every summer after. I really didn't have a choice. "Freier men work!" Dad often repeated. So, my eleven-year-old head nodded and moved forward. So, I guess that's what we do. Work. Drive. Achieve.

I had learned to show up to the world, vowing to get what I wanted from others and from situations. It was a transactional life. While it was plainly obvious to others that behind my drive was an insecure little boy longing for attention, I was oblivious. Have you been driven by a need for validation or even just to be seen? That was me. I couldn't be stopped, so I just kept pushing.

Parenthetically, some may be thinking, "Wait, didn't you grow up in a home of faith? Didn't you worship each week?" Yes! However, the overriding theology in my parochial worldview was grounded with a premise which we confessed every Sunday, "I, a poor miserable sinner, confess unto Thee all my sins and iniquities with which I have ever offended Thee and justly deserved Thy temporal and eternal punishment. But I am heartily sorry for them and sincerely repent of them..." What's a kid who feels emotionally abandoned supposed to do with that weekly mantra? Developmentally, I couldn't process it. The negative feelings connected with "who I was" never went away. This young, "poor miserable sinner" showed up at home and worship services each week and wondered what it meant to be accepted and loved unconditionally. So I lived with the dilemma that, because of some divine mercy (at times even seen as pity), I would go to heaven, but, until then, "I kinda sucked, unless I could prove otherwise." This was another integral part in forming a transaction mentality for me.

The foundational theme of my story was posing and acting. I became a professional poser. I wasn't really vulnerable or real. My relationships were based on transactions, and I was just going through the motions.

Through all of this, though I learned valuable lessons of hard work, perseverance, striving for excellence, and how to be comfortable with all different types of people, it didn't matter if I walked into a room of strangers or found myself on stage; I learned to lean into the discomfort and do my best. I could adapt to almost any situation and, most of the time, have fun with whomever I was with and whatever we did. These skills still serve me well.

Breathe and Pause

What is your story?

How do you interpret your wounds?

What is the go-to message of your inner critic?

What vows or agreements have you made?

We grow up in a sea of stories told in a way that fits what we want others to know about us. The stories told in most families are a kind of propaganda. The tragedy is that often these stories are simply a form of dis-information. –DAN ALLENDER

CHAPTER 2

Uncovering Story Themes

Many denominations traditionally celebrate eighth-grade confirmation. It didn't mean much to me. Preadolescents don't take life too seriously. I memorized all the verses, facts, and hymns the fastest and enjoyed my party and the money in the cards from my relatives. A special part of the ceremony happens when the pastor, in this case my dad, reads a Bible passage over you. I vaguely remember it. *I am not ashamed of the Gospel, it is the power of God* (Romans 1:16). I didn't realize this would start a four-year repetitive cycle of divine words that, looking back, I needed to hear and understand.

High school was all about building and maintaining an image. Although I was scrawny, I did my best to engage in athletic activities. If I couldn't win on the athletic field, I would win through articulation, humor, sarcasm, and musically outperforming others. I discovered that transactional living also worked when dating. I knew what I wanted, and I understood what my dates could provide. In my mind, it was a win-win. In reality, it was a win-lose proposition.

My high school sweetheart and now wife of four decades (you must be wondering what she was thinking) told me before we started dating, "I don't like you. I will not date you nor become one of the female statistics in your life." Challenge accepted!

The Harsh Realities of Story Themes

I showed up, but it was plainly evident to others that much of my life was a charade. I was still getting in trouble at home; spankings turned to regular groundings. The expression of negative emotions was forbidden, so I swallowed my fear, anger, and sadness into an ulcer. So I performed with more intensity. The accolades, ovations, and plaques couldn't sooth my soul. Yet posing and performing were all I knew. And I became even better at them both.

I WAS A LIVING FABLE, ONE THAT I ALLOWED OTHER PEOPLE TO WRITE.

I was a living fable, one that I allowed other people to write. That may sound harsh, but that is reality. Brené Brown puts it this way, "If we don't own our story we end up 'hustling for worthiness' on the outside of our story—who we are and what we believe become secondary to who you want me to be and what you want me to believe" (*The Hustle for Worthiness* DVD).

Four years of riding the wave of popularity and getting what I needed to survive came to a screeching halt at the end of my senior year of high school. I had no idea what I wanted to do with my life. I repeatedly vowed, or swore, that I would never enter the family business and become a pastor. That left the career field wide open. Or so I thought. What I soon realized is that when you grow up in a very small parochial world, with regular doses of career advice from a father that he repeated at home and in public—"The highest calling in life was to be a pastor"—your subconsciousness and consciousness collide. My *move against* became paralyzed. I was clueless.

During my senior year, I turned to my football coach—who was also a pastor—for advice. Here's the interchange.

"What do you want to do, Mark?"

"I donna know. I think be a high school teacher or counselor. Maybe an EMT."

"Well, to be a high school teacher in our denomination, you have to be a pastor."

"That sucks! I don't want to be a pastor. So now what?"

"Well, I think you should become a pastor and keep the field open."

I felt like burnt toast. What's a poser to do? When you are a fraud and you feel like your back is against the wall and you don't have the good sense to know whom to fight or what to fight for, you acquiesce. It means you accept something reluctantly, but without protest. I protested all right, but only internally. The theme for the next season of my life became built on the first. I was still posing, but I showed up as complying.

For our high school graduation, the class officers chose a Bible verse to be our theme: *I am not ashamed of the Gospel, it is the power of God* (Romans 1:16). Same verse…odd, indeed.

Three months later, my family drove me six hours to a small preministerial college in mid-Wisconsin. I hated the whole ordeal. I hated packing. I hated not knowing what I wanted to do with my life. I hated going to an all-male school. I hated that it was a preministerial college. I hated the culture. I hated leaving my high school sweetheart, probably the one thing in this life up to that point that I didn't hate. Did I mention that I hated…pretty much everything?

I was entering a college curriculum based on the German gymnasium (schools with a rigorous academic learning emphasis including a study of classical languages): twenty-one mandatory credit hours each semester of Latin, German, Greek, and Hebrew. The environment was laden with sarcasm and mockery. Athletic prowess was the highest honor. What you did mattered more than who you were. And being able to outdrink classmates was the prize. Bars were on almost every corner of this small Wisconsin town. The men in our school did our best to fill them. It was a different form of transactional living. Yet transactional, indeed. I had to learn a new way to survive. So I continued to pose as a small fish in a bigger pond, and I learned how to comply, which really meant to figure out how to not get in trouble (i.e., not to get kicked out of school).

I struggled academically. In the first semester, the dean of students told me to switch to the five-year plan because I was so behind in my language preparation (none of which I had gotten in high school.) Another year was not an option. It would not only mean failure; worse, it would mean another year of torture at the hellhole of a school. I accepted the challenge to pass my classes. So I trudged through. There were a few bright moments where I could apply my musical talents on stage. However, almost every part of it was drudgery, humiliation, and survival. I had the lowest GPA allowed to graduate. At the graduation service, there was a banner of the class Bible verse that hung above our heads; it read, *I am not ashamed of the Gospel, it is the power of God* (Romans 1:16). I didn't notice. I should have. It wasn't as if God wasn't trying to show me. It was proof that I certainly wasn't self-aware.

What does a twenty-one-year-old with a bachelor of liberal arts with an emphasis in Greek and Hebrew do with his life? Well, one of my classmates became a professor of Hebrew at the University of Wisconsin. Not my career path. I came home for the summer to work, realizing that most of my classmates were going to the seminary north of Milwaukee to get a master's degree in divinity. Yikes! In full complying mode, I packed my bags for another four years of classical-languages and doctrine classes.

The first year of seminary was a continuation of college. Have you ever felt stuck in Groundhog Day? Poor academics and lots of drinking. For reasons beyond my comprehension, my high school sweetheart changed her mind, became my fiancée, and accepted my marriage proposal. However, as the summer approached and wedding plans were in full swing, moments of maturity blossomed. I knew she deserved better than an academic ingrate and self-absorbed person who readily complied.

Why Would My Wife Want to Be a Part of My Story?

Friends still ask her that question. I've learned not to shrink in embarrassment when it's asked. Deb came from a home where she was deeply loved and where her self-worth was nurtured. She wasn't impressed by my EGO-driven shenanigans. Yet I was a bit of an enigma to her. As I reflect on it, I think that her kind, compassionate presence had a way of softening my hardened heart. The more we spent time together, the more I slowly let down my walls. As I did so, she began to see me for who I was, someone who had the potential of being passionate, as well as kind. "Potential" is the operative word. Deb believed in me when I could not and did not believe in myself. She was the first female since third grade who looked me in the eyes and smiled. She wanted to spend time with me. She wanted to hold my hand. She even delighted in me, whether it was laughing at my goofiness or celebrating lame waterskiing tricks. When we were separated by hundreds of miles for five years when I was in school, she wrote beautiful letters to me. They were love letters in the truest definition of the word "love": vulnerable, compassionate, and honest. I began to believe what she was writing about us, about me. I couldn't ignore her. I didn't want to. I was drawn to her. I wanted to spend the rest of my life with her.

The Memorable Day

Thanks to Debbie's vision of a wedding celebration and our desire for a wedding ceremony that was spectacular, every part of the day was memorable. For the first time in my life, it wasn't all about me. I wanted Deb to be happy and to feel special. What I knew for sure is that this kind, generous, gregarious, and gorgeous woman was someone who had made a commitment to love me. And the unconditional love I received from her was something I had never experienced before. To be honest, I was overwhelmed by it.

For the next three years at the seminary, I was determined to apply myself. Deb studied with me; she encouraged me and stood by me, as I slowly embraced the potential of a career as a pastor. I could feel the tides shifting inside of me. I didn't have a name for the theme then, but I do now, I was moving into a **striving theme**, while having almost perfected posing and complying. I had something I didn't have before. I had a goal. I had someone to fight for and something to move against. My spirit was coming back.

The third year of seminary is the time when you intern. I was fortunate to get a supervisor who was a hard driver, who expected excellence and gave me enough freedom to excel. For the first time in years, that is what happened. Those years of being on stage and performing allowed me to show up being comfortable in front of people, whether a few dozen or a few hundred. I realized that I had an affinity for teenagers and helping them navigate the insecurities and uncertainties of their world. Apparently, I could relate.

We also had our first child that year, Anne. Things were falling into place; my wife was glowing and loved being a mom; I was doing well as an intern; and we were a family.

The last year of seminary was a grind. I went from doing ministry and succeeding in it to sitting in classrooms for two full semesters, rehashing more languages, church history, and doctrine. After one more year of complying, I could put the afterburners into building my career by striving.

Graduating from seminary is an odd adventure. Not the graduation part, but the assignment part. You don't search for a job. Rather, you are assigned a congregation somewhere in the world to serve. You can decline a foreign position. Other than that, you get what you get. As "call day" (what it's called) approached, it was as if a switch flipped from complying to striving. I went into full-bore EGO-driven mode. After all, I had survived twenty years of parochial school, and it was time for me to get what I wanted – a transactional belief. Quid pro quo! Plain and simple. If I had to be a pastor (nice choice of words for myself), there were three pastoral things I did not want. Transactional thinking dies hard for us stubborn people. One, I did not want to be near Milwaukee, the headquarters of our denomination. Two, I did not want to be in a large congregation. Three, I did not want to be an associate pastor. It turned out that what I didn't want was telling God exactly what I needed. Tell God what you DON'T want, and there is a good chance that God will make sure you get the lesson that comes with all that you think. Guess what? I got all three.

To top it off, the class officers had chosen a verse as our class motto. You'll never guess, *I am not ashamed of the Gospel, it is the power of God* (Romans 1:16). That's intriguing!

Now, every four years, over twelve years, this Bible verse gets front and center. I would like to tell you that, by this time, it was clear: the divine revelation had enlightened me, and I deeply changed. Such is not the case. We rarely move or notice those pieces until we look back later.

Let me share with you what I know now that I wish I would have known then.

What I interpreted this verse to mean—which, by the way, is a total misrepresentation of the intent—is based on a warped equation manufactured by my dysfunctions. The first variable of the equation was my childhood message from my dad: being a pastor was "the highest calling." The second variable was the message throughout my preministerial training: a pastor has "spiritual authority," and people need to "submit to that authority." The final variable of the equation is that I associated the Gospel with the word power: pastors had the power to preach, making the position of pastor powerful. I don't like to admit it; this became a subconscious vow I made as to how I would show up in my career. I had learned to pose to hide this vow, but let me assure you it was plainly evident to anyone who spent some time around me that there was something going on beneath the surface.

I interpreted the job of a pastor combined with the verse to mean that, as a pastor, I should not be afraid to pursue the highest calling of preaching and wield spiritual authority, because I get to share the power of the Gospel. I had a new-found authority. Close, but no cigar! Alan Fadling's conviction is clear, "Legitimate authority and genuine honor are always given" (*An Unhurried Life*). I wanted to seize power. This verse isn't the authority of a pastor or anything to do with my power; it's about the Gospel. Furthermore, the nuance of the verse is that the Gospel is powerful.

So what is the Gospel? When you ask most churchgoers the question, they answer with some reference to what an itinerate rabbi came and did over two thousand years ago. That answers the question of what this rabbi did, but it leaves out the why. Why did Jesus do what He did? What is the why of God? How does God really view me? This touches my core.

Because of the weekly religious ritual repeating that I was a poor miserable sinner (missing that I was deeply loved by God), I developed a perverted belief system: God is disgusted with me, annoyed with me, and, at best, tolerates me. Because He has mercy, He must forgive me, and even though He might, He still is annoyed with who I am. Unlike Mr. Rogers, God could never sing to me, "It's you I like…"

The transactional belief system of my childhood was colliding with the transactional belief system of a young man. The core of the Gospel and the core teaching of Jesus was not that I was that poor miserable sinner. It was instead this: God loves me. I am God's Beloved. After all, *God is love* (I John 4). This is what I had to learn, and I had to learn it in real time, while I was in the midst of a career where this is what I'm supposed to confidently tell people: I should never be ashamed of the simple, true, and clear message of divine love. God is love; it is good news. In that simple message is power. I am not the power. My sharing it is not the power. My charisma is not the power. My talents are not the power. The church is not the power. My position is not the power. The power is love. Never be ashamed of THAT.

Breath and Pause

What are the themes of your story?
How do these themes show up in your life?
Is there a divine message that is driving you?

When people alter their interior world, they also alter their exterior world. –ROBERT E. QUINN

Our ability to grow as a leader is based on our ability to grow as a person. –KEVIN KUSHMAN

CHAPTER 3

What's Really Happening Inside

At twenty-five years old, I became the pastor of youth and family ministry at one of the most influential congregations in the denomination. It was an associate pastor position just a few miles from the denomination's headquarters, a large area Lutheran high school, and Wisconsin Lutheran College. There were seventeen denomination officials and professors in our congregation. Yeah! I got what I didn't want and exactly what I needed.

The next four years were a steep learning curve and introduced me to the idea of "transformation." It comes from the Greek word *metamorphosis*—a change of being. It turns out that God is all about transformation. It's a transformation of the mind so that we think about things that are good and noble. It's a transformation of the heart so that we have more grace and act with kindness toward others. Transformation is literally a change of mind and heart. It happens over time, and it occurs from the inside out. It's not behavior modification. It's an intentional process of training to learn how to love others, as we learn to love ourselves. Wow! Life is not about making transactions; it's about living transformationally.

> TRANSFORMATION IS LITERALLY A CHANGE OF MIND AND HEART.

It would have been devasting to be placed in a congregation by myself at that point in my life. That's why I loathed getting the associate pastor position, but I needed it so desperately. Out of the gate, internally I saw myself as an assistant, not an associate. The word "associate" implies "being equal to," while the word "assistant" has a narrower scope and means that one is still learning. I had the title of "associate," but, too many times, I showed up with an "assistant" mentality.

My associate, Ron Hines, was so different from me, yet so good for me. In so many ways and at so many levels, he shaped me: planting seeds in my mind that broadened my outlook of what life and serving people could be, challenging me to think outside of the box, giving me a forum where excellence was demanded and grace was extended, watching how essential it was to stand on principles instead of caving in or giving in just to avoid conflict (being a peacemaker not a peacekeeper), ruthlessly guarding family time, inviting me to conversations with people who also would challenge me, and the freedom to see what could happen if we just tried doing ministry and trusted the process. He was a coworker and, more important, a coach, and, eventually, a mentor. I am truly grateful.

My position at this congregation was created to find out

why kids, after eighth-grade confirmation, were apathetic, bored and turned off by God. They had the data to prove it. Although they didn't need the data, it was commonly known that such was the case. My outcome objective was to find out why and fix it. It's like they were sweet-talking my *move against* style of relating. Challenge accepted!

The problem was a pretty easy diagnosis. We started examining the curriculum and teaching style in the Lutheran elementary school. Religion had been a subject to study and learn and to regurgitate facts. The smart ones got good grades and the rest were…well, they just got poorer grades and were less honored. It was all about knowledge (transaction) and not about the heart (transformation). Kids were made to feel guilty—more precisely, shamed—into behaving correctly. It was becoming painfully obvious that kids were being taught that WHAT they knew and did mattered more than WHO they were. Wait a minute! I knew that approach. I understood that approach. I lived that approached. We were training children to become transactional people. Crap!

In addition, most parents had relegated the teaching of anything religious to the experts. They treated religious education like dropping off the kids to a soccer coach. Teach my kids to be religious, and it doesn't matter WHO we are or WHAT we do at home. Just do your job.

Here I am, a young pastor who was tasked with fixing a problem of monumental proportion. I didn't have a clue about the next step, so I just started talking about it. Deep inside, I wondered who would listen. I still felt like there was nothing that I could offer, but I spoke up anyway. Turns out, the seventeen denominational officials and professors at the high school and college were ready to listen. Were my ideas dumb?

Nope! They listened. They were intrigued, and they wanted to be a part of the solution.

Over the next four years, we challenged the status quo of how to teach religion, how to discipline children, how to raise children, and much more. We implemented a new curriculum that focused on teaching to both the head and the heart. Parents and teachers were taught a new way of relating to children by creating a nurturing and loving environment designed to dignify children, to enliven their faith, and to enlarge their heart.

During this time, we welcomed our second daughter, Katie, into our family. I am embarrassed to think about how much I let my career consume my time and energy during these important years. I put Debbie in the position of feeling like a single mom.

Daring to Look Inside

In so many ways, I had been prepared to stand in front of people, to teach, to encourage, and even to inspire them. And I was being noticed. The accolades and ovations that had eluded me in college and seminary reappeared with a vengeance. I was becoming a big fish in a small pond. My striving theme was being fueled by admiration, winning, and doing better than others.

What I wasn't prepared for was what the public ministry was doing to me. I was gradually becoming distant from my family, leaving Deb with most of the household chores and raising the girls. All the work, all the exposure, was draining me and fueling my EGO. It was breeding a level of narcissism and grandiosity and their offspring, entitlement, rage, boredom, and so on. I hid most of it well. I showed up and put on a good front, and it was plainly evident to Deb that she and the kids were paying for my success.

At moments, when I was tired and exhausted, I found myself at both ends of the continuum: "I'm great!" and "I suck!" I had pledged allegiance to the Gospel of dynamic power but had taken on the role that I would be a generator of power. After all, my career was the "highest calling." I had adopted an ancillary darker philosophy that everyone in business had lower callings and that while they made money, it was to support those of us with the "highest calling—we were doing God's work." I know, it's demented. This was the not-so-subtle message I repeatedly heard during those formable years. The transformation we each go through doesn't come easy, and it isn't usually instant, either.

On the outside, for the most part, I had it together. I was doing the right things—praying and reading Scripture, as well as a host of authors from various disciplines. However, the real horror was how easy it was for me to remain in a comfortable, distorted illusion I didn't have the courage or skill to face. I didn't take the time, and I didn't know how to look deep inside my interior, my heart.

> "WHO YOU ARE LEAKS...AND HAS MORE LONG-TERM INFLUENCE THAN ANYTHING YOU DO."

I had lots of experience managing my image. I was under the impression that this was all that really mattered. I was posing to have it all together, yet I was leaking something entirely different. Today, I call it "The Principle of the Leak," which I learned from my friend, Ron Martoia (Morph), "Who you are leaks...and has more long-term influence than anything you do." Yikes! It is usually unconscious and unintentional; its effects are more pervasive than your words, and it starts from the inside out.

Here's the analogy. Growing up in southwest Michigan, I remember the sights, smells, and events of the fall. From harvest days to apple picking, from walks on the piers to bonfires, it's just a great time of year. Another scene I remember is the time when the marinas take in the boats for winter storage. During the boating season, we see the top side: the shine, the amenities, and the uniqueness of each watercraft. Each fall season exposes another essential function of the boat— unseen in the water but critical to its success. Laymen call it the "underside"; most know it as the hull. Each form has a unique shape that gives it certain handling and performance characteristics. But one thing is certain: the hull is of utmost importance. Leaks occur from the underside. And we leak from the inside out.

The repeated emphasis from anyone who talks about or writes about Transformational Leadership is the importance of intentionally focusing on inner transformation— life below the waterline. Ken Blanchard (*The Secret: What Great Leaders Know—and Do*) paints the picture of an iceberg and its makeup below the surface. Here is the graphic we use at Nexecute to teach the foundational principles of Transformational Leadership:

The implications are clear: be aware of your inner life—life below the waterline. Only 10 percent of the iceberg is above the water. In terms of life, it is what other people see. Although this might seem odd, most of our life is spent in making sure that we function well above the waterline. IQ and skills matter. However, in the scheme of things, it is the easy work.

The hard work is the work below the waterline. This is our

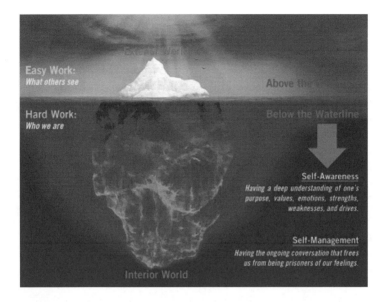

interior world. Because people can function and, by some measure, succeed by only focusing on the exterior world, that is the go-to for most people. America is built on the premise of takeover, siege, and competition. Winning is the standard. Silver and bronze are technically seen as 1st and 2nd place losers. With this overemphasis on achievement, the interior world is virtually ignored—that is, until there are moral failures, severe illnesses, broken relationships, burnouts, or indictments that are the results of ignoring the inner world.

I was introduced to this analogy years ago. At times, I've been uniquely aware of it, and, at other times, I've sadly ignored the principles. However, my alignment doesn't change the time-tested truth. I'm just asked to make the choice to live according to what is right and what ultimately works.

Over a decade ago, Dee Hock, founder and former CEO of the VISA credit card association rocked the leadership world when he proposed that if leaders truly understood the system they were asked to lead, they would make the unconventional choice to manage the right people with the right energy. He suggested that leaders spend at least 40 percent of their time managing themselves. How could this be with deadlines and profits hanging in the balance? He wrote, in *The Art of Chaordic Leadership*, "The first and paramount responsibility of anyone who purports to manage (or lead) is to manage self: one's own integrity, character, ethics, knowledge, wisdom, temperament, words, and acts. It is a complex, unending incredibly difficult, oft-shunned task. We spend little time and rarely excel at self-management precisely because it is much more difficult than prescribing and controlling the behavior of others. However, without management of self, no one is fit for authority no matter how much they acquire, for the more authority they acquire the more dangerous they become."

We continue to see today, in business, athletics, politics, and life, the destructive results of people who have gotten more authority and who, because they have ignored their interior world, have become more dangerous.

Those are poignant words for anyone in any type of leadership position. It tends to be a bit easier and certainly quicker to spit and polish the surface materials—our persona. The difficult work of our inner world doesn't respond to a quick fix.

Making the choice to spend time below the waterline means focusing on two keys areas: self-awareness and self-management. How do you do that?

Practicing Self-Awareness and Self-Management

Step #1: Self-Awareness. Tasha Eurich calls self-awareness "the meta-skill of the 21st Century." (Insight) At that time in my life, I didn't realize it was a skill to possess, much less learn. Eurich candidly states, "For most people, it's easier to choose self-delusion—the antithesis of self-awareness—over the cold, hard truth." I had to learn, in real time and without much guidance (her book would be written decades later), how to make the arduous journey from self-delusion to self-awareness.

First, it's about noticing feelings. This may seem odd; however, it is essential to start there. I entered adulthood with no effective emotional vocabulary. So it seemed peculiar to me to name emotions. My counselor introduced me to a very simple tool: a Feeling Wheel. It may sound absurd—to see feelings written on a color coded visual—but, for me, I needed that rudimentary beginning. I had to stop, to reflect, and, then, to allow myself to feel. The next step was having the courage to name the emotion—actually asking yourself, "What am I feeling?" Sure, there are the basic emotions of being sad, being mad, being scared, being peaceful, being powerful, and being joyful. But there are many layers—stronger and weaker—around each of these emotions. Once I noticed and named my emotions, I could then begin to understand my triggers—the strong emotional responses to situations—people or events—when things got tough, when things got frustrating, or when things didn't go my way. Why is this so important?

This is what happened to me when I didn't possess the skill of this first step. I remember being part of a retreat with a staff that was designed to build trust and to deal with the overt and covert conflict of the team. Halfway through the retreat, the facilitator said to me, "Mark, you use the word 'frustrated' a lot to describe your emotions around this team." I shrugged. He continued, "Frustration is really a layer of anger. It seems to me that you have a lot of buried anger." I was stunned.

"You should deal with that anger sometime." I knew that deep within me was a cauldron of anger. It repeatedly boiled to the surface with inconsistent bursts and without commitment or purpose. Often, my intense response did not match the situation. Therefore, people were stunned by my overactions. Repeatedly, I got embarrassed and tried ever harder to control them. My attempts to fix these "leaks" were only dealing with the symptoms. I had not dealt with the heart of what was causing those leaks. Desperate for clarity, I retorted, "How about now?" I wasn't anticipating that he would agree and lead me through this exercise in front of the team. He asked me to verbalize my anger. "Put words to it!" Twice, I tried to muster up words or phrases to tap into my anger. None of the team were convinced. He then asked someone to throw me a coat. "Mark, your hands are very expressive," he stated. "I want you to channel your emotion of anger into your hands. Go ahead. Let 'er rip!" I was told that, for over fifteen minutes, I wept, as I let my hands express my anger. Clenching! Twisting! Tightening! Until I could grasp it no longer. Again, he concluded, "There's a lot of anger, Mark. You might want to explore that further." At that point in my life, I didn't have the courage or humility to do so. How I wish I would have. What I didn't know then is that he was leading me into the next step.

THE TRUTH IS THAT IF WE DON'T DEAL WITH OUR PAIN, OUR BODY WILL HOLD THE PAIN, AND WE WILL TRANSMIT IT TO OTHER PEOPLE.

Step #2: Self-Management. Emotions are good information. They are data that give you insight. Ask yourself, "WHY am I reacting the way I do; what is my motivation?" We often tend to avoid the motivation behind our feelings because it is more normal, and, frankly, easier, to just react. The deeper reason to avoid this step is that we think it will be too painful. The truth is that if we don't deal with our pain, our body will hold the pain, and we will transmit it to other people. The transmission of pain is damaging to every one of our relationships. We end up reacting—exuding a negative force of self-protection—instead of responding with mindfulness. Motivation questions can be as simple as

- Why am I so anxious?

- Why am I feeling courageous?

- Why am I overly concerned that others tell me I'm okay as a leader?

- Why am I so grateful?

- Why do I find myself apologizing about so many things?

These type of questions (there are dozens more) are a means toward self-discovery. It's not about overanalyzing or ruminating on them. It's learning about ourselves. Remembering to face the "cold, hard truth."

When you accept your reality by asking motivating questions you are now prepared to ask the all-important parallel question of self-management. It's the action question. "What do you want to do differently next time?" By asking yourself this action question, you will give yourself the dignity and space of examining the past and envisioning the future. It will waylay any tendency to ruminate and challenge the downward spiral toward a victim mindset. It will propel you to self-empowerment. It will remind you that the ball is squarely in your court. It will give you the opportunity to decide how you want to show up moving forward.

Breathe and Pause

What are the temptations that feed your EGO?

Who has paid or is currently paying for the time and energy you are putting into building your success?

What are you leaking? What is the impact on others?

What have you noticed about your desire and approach to managing yourself?

Take the Thirty-Day Challenge. Practice the steps of Self-Awareness and Self-Management and ask the pertinent questions in each step. For 30 days, take four minutes each day and reflect—possibly Journal—on strong emotions you had that day and ask yourself "Why" you reacted the way you did. In doing so, you are beginning to engrain a habit of mindfulness called "noticing." Take the final minute to ask yourself the action question, "What do I want to do differently next time?"

*EGO has a voracious appetite, the more you feed it,
the hungrier it gets. –*NATHAN BRONNER

*You can either be a host to God, or a hostage to your EGO.
It's your call. –*WAYNE DYER

CHAPTER 4

The Fall of a Kingdom

Life and death happen to all of us. Deb had had a miscarriage.
It seems like it just happens, and you move on. There wasn't
any space to grieve. I didn't realize that I was missing that
space because I didn't know what questions to ask myself. It
seemed that people didn't talk much about having a miscarriage. It's like it happened and then you just move on. Isn't
there any space to grieve? I remember a couple of days later
making a shut-in call to a wonderful, elderly gentlemen and
sharing with him the news of the miscarriage. I started weep-
ing. It took me off guard. I wasn't prepared for such a display
of vulnerability. Yet, at a small kitchen table in a century-old
house, this elderly gentleman and I cried together at the
sadness of life and the missed opportunity of being a father
again. Sitting with that man was the start of a conversation I
needed to have with myself. Would I take the time to explore

it further? Unfortunately, no. Instead I ignored the space that had been created in the kitchen that day and picked up my life right where it left off.

What does an unhealed transactional person do when he or she experiences success in one location? Trick question. He doesn't allow himself to feel success, because there must be something more. So he starts looking. You didn't? I did!

A close friend warned me not to take the position of senior pastor of a church in Michigan. He strongly told me that my doing so would be about building my kingdom and my EGO. I told myself that this once-proud congregation needed someone strong to bring the dying church back to life. Something to fight for? Challenge accepted!

Deb was ready to go for very different reasons. She was hopeful that getting me out of the fishbowl that was our current professional and personal life would rescue us; she would get her husband back, and our girls would finally have someone who was present for them instead of for everyone else.

I showed up in Michigan, ready to make a difference and to make this fledgling church alive again. On my first tour of the campus, we walked into an empty facility, and I heard an EGO-stroking statement, "Your job is to fill these pews again." Challenge accepted!

Applying every conceivable thing I had learned, I implemented changes quickly and without regard to whoever got in the way. People tried to get in the way. and I just mowed them over. I won't bore you with the details, but the congregation turned around. Every data point in every area saw double-digit growth. From the outside, things were rocking. New members were joining.

I also learned to spend time with Deb and the girls, and

we welcomed our son, Nathan, into our family. We built some fond memories together. I was learning how to engage with my family: playing, laughing, walking, having little adventures in the woods, playing catch, and more. We created some fond memories, but I had a lot more to learn in this area.

Things were going well at home, and work was flourishing. At least, that is what I thought.

The Enneagram is a dynamic, ancient personality tool which reveals how we take in information, how we process that information, and also how we relate to others. It's a great self-awareness tool that reveals different patterns of thinking, feeling, and acting that arise from a deeper inner motivation or worldview. It's a convicting tool. It reveals how we approach life from our EGO—a transactional mind-set. Further study of the Enneagram reveals how a transformational person approaches life with the same number but with an entirely different mind-set, yielding positive results flowing from insight, love, and grace.

According to the Enneagram, I am a 3—Achiever (no surprise). Transactionally, it means that winning is all about me. The basic desire is to feel valuable. There is a need for endless successes and feedback to reassure me against a very honest and realistic insecurity. The blind spot for an Achiever is deceit. That's important because, during all the success of this new church transformation, I was blinded by deceit. I was unaware of the unhappiness that lay just beneath the facade I had created. That there was an influential group of people, along with my associate pastor, who were not just unhappy; they also wanted to get rid of me.

Out of the blue, a senior leader in the church scheduled an appointment with me and quickly began to ask probing and accusatory questions about my approach to and style of ministry. At a subsequent appointment, he revealed that he had been doing research and had found out that I was operating on the fringes of what was proper for the denomination, and he said that it would no longer be tolerated at this congregation; He concluded, "You are going down." I am not proud of what I did; it is what it is. I was EGO-driven; an Achiever (Type 3, Enneagram), combined with a *move against* mindset. I fed into all of my insecurities and challenge that I heard in his words and replied with, "Oh yeah? Go ahead and try to take me down."

The next months were brutal. Brutal for my family, brutal for the people I led, and brutal for me. There were clandestine evening meetings at a local business to pour over the antagonist's findings. Unbeknownst to me, there were clandestine meetings between my superiors conspiring against me. Speaking engagements around the denomination dried up. Training videos I had done for our denomination were eventually banned, because my teaching was suspect. I was labeled, and I was literally going down. My influence was waning. I was under attack after every class I taught and every message I preached.

My kingdom crumbled in every way. I was defeated and in despair. My insecurity was exposed.

It became apparent to me that I was losing the fight, so my *move against* retreated. I focused on my family, played racquetball for hours a day, and spent the rest of the week dejected, depressed, and depleted. I showed up to events as a mere shell, and it was plainly obvious to people that things were not right. I was transmitting my pain in almost every situation. I was really going down.

Breathe and Pause

How have you been tempted to act out of building your EGO?

How do you react when things don't go your way?

Change is inevitable. Growth is optional. –JOHN C. MAXWELL

Transformation isn't sweet and bright. It's a dark and murky, painful pushing. An unraveling of the untruths you've carried in your body. A practice in facing your own created demons. A complete uprooting, before becoming. –VICTORIA ERICKSON

CHAPTER 5

Good 'Ole Country Western Blues Song

My wife's style of relating is *move toward*. She prefers to be around a small group of people she really trusts. She also knows how to create healthy boundaries. She became more and more skeptical of the people in that Michigan congregation and felt there was no one she could trust. Deb knew that a boundary had to be drawn for her flailing husband. She engaged in hard conversations with me about moving to a new position or out of ministry altogether. She was strong and serious.

It turned out that one of pastor friends in Coral Springs, Florida, wanted to introduce a new innovative approach in his congregation. He heard about my challenges and was able to get a three-year grant that would fund my position. I was numb. Deb ultimately made the decision that it was time to move, and to move far away from the Midwest and to try something different.

It was a positive move for so many reasons. We had a fresh start. People were happy to see us and warmly welcomed us. They facilitated the purchase and preparation of our first home, so no more parsonage (a house provided for the clergy) life. South Florida was green, warm (hot), close to the ocean, and provided hours of outside activities. It was a healing time for our marriage, our family, and for me professionally.

In that professional respect, it was difficult to get back into the swing of things. However, years of striving were embedded in the synapses of my brain, and it didn't take long before they began to fire again. And with that came a measured level of success. I was aware, though, that I could not approach work at the expense of my family. And I didn't. We camped, rollerbladed, rode bikes, swam, and soaked up all that South Florida had to offer. This included taking multiple trips to Walt Disney World, which afforded me the opportunity to experience the by-product of a company that was intentional about its purpose and core values. I became a fan for many reasons and, eventually, a student of its methodologies.

I started to experience something that was foreign to me: self-awareness. I couldn't have named the phenomenon. I certainly didn't have the understanding or expertise to act on it. I was a fledgling in this new arena.

Peter Scazzero, author of *Emotionally Healthy Spirituality* and *The Emotionally Healthy Church*, had not written about emotional and spiritual health in the early 1990s. I wonder what I would have done with the following quotation from

"Ignoring our emotions is turning our back on reality." one of his books. My guess is that it would have been hard for me to swallow his haunting words, "Ignoring our emotions is turning our back on reality."

Reckoning with the Truth

Like any achiever, I figured that this whole transformational process should not be approached in a half-assed way. If I were going to engage with the process, it would take a full commitment, no holding back. Just before my 38th birthday, I had lunch with a small group of people at a small Fort Lauderdale diner to hear about transformation—changing from the inside out. I only remember one sentence of the lunch, "Humility is the pathway to intimacy with God." That struck a chord deep within me. I knew I wasn't humble, and, certainly, didn't have a clue about how to pursue God. My God experience was mainly an intellectual assent. I could talk about God and, if needed, I could debate about God. But intimacy with God wasn't a phrase I used or understood. I remember that day, almost in a cavalier attitude, I said, "What the heck. I am not humble, and I don't know intimacy with God. So, God, whatever it takes to make me humble, go ahead." When I share this part of my story, people gasp and, with eyes wide open, often respond, "You didn't say that, did you?" Yes, I did, for, over forty-five days in a row, that was my mantra, my prayer. After all, what's the worst that can happen? God accepted the challenge!

What I write next is an encapsulated version of the next two years of my life. The reality is a complex and layered, emotionally charged time. There are stories and realities that only my family and certain friends can truly know and understand. I called out to God, asked to be humbled, and here is the response. Without rhyme, but with the despair and tears of a Good Ole' Country western tune, I share the timeline of loss that happened next.

Verse One

On day forty-five, my life would change.

I left the denomination of my youth: my pension, my insurance, and my relational identity.

My extended family is deeply hurt and doesn't know how to relate to me,

Abandoned again.

I took a 35 percent cut in pay,

Was diagnosed with thyroid cancer and had a thyroidectomy,

Went through radioactive iodine treatment to eradicate my thyroid,

Gained over thirty pounds.

I was unable to work or perform chores, and that forced me to be dependent on others.

Chorus

I began to realize that my life was a gift,

And that, maybe, just maybe,

> *Love was the key,*

> *And that life wasn't all about me.*

My wife and children loved me deeply, and we grew close.

Humility was happening without my effort.

Verse Two

Returning to work was a slow process.

What seemed to matter more than achieving was

Relationships,

Love,

Family,

Laughter.

While I respected my friend who had brought us to Florida, we parted ways, and I lost my job,

Which meant no income, no money, and being totally dependent on others for survival.

Chorus

I began to realize that my life was a gift,

And that, maybe, just maybe,

> *Love was the key,*

> *And that life wasn't all about me.*

My wife and children loved me deeply, and we grew close.

Humility was happening without my effort.

Verse Three

The only viable job offer was back in Michigan,

Which meant a cross-country move with two preadolescents who didn't want to leave their close friends and the home they loved.

I couldn't sooth their pain or stop their tears.

The only place we could afford to live was in the basement of an old farmhouse:

Spiderwebs, mold, and one bathroom for two families.

The pain continued when our only dog, ironically named Angel, was hit by a school bus in front of our eyes.

We buried her amidst tears of pain and sorrow.

Relationships in the house began to unravel, so we moved again,

This time into the home of another family.

Another thyroid-cancer screen added twenty pounds more.

It would be well over a year before we had our own place to live in.

Chorus
I began to realize that my life was a gift,

And that, maybe, just maybe,

Love was the key,

And that life wasn't all about me.

My wife and children loved me deeply, and we grew close.

Humility was happening without my effort.

What a ride! My family paid a dear price for me to learn a lesson. I can tell you that on the other side of pain was healing, growth, and, yes, transformation. And we will not change until the pain on the outside matches the pain on the inside. I had so much pain. So much had to heal. It was a process of learning, at every level of my life.

When I share this story, some brave souls will respond with something like, "I want to be where you are without going through the pain of what you went through." I look them squarely in the eye and, with compassion, say, "Then I would begin to practice self-awareness and self-management. Know your story. Uncover the messages you use to cope with your wounds and speak the agreements you made in the darkness into the light. Because that which is the light has more power than that which is in the darkness." Few choose that path.

Breathe and Pause

How are you doing at knowing your story, finding the truth and the fables?

How comfortable are you with your emotions?

What are you noticing about what you are thinking and feeling?

If we don't transform our pain, we will most assuredly transmit it. Transformation is often more about unlearning than learning. –RICHARD ROHR

CHAPTER 6

From Transmitting to Transforming

After a two-year roller-coaster ride like that, we all needed to get our bearings. We spent time together working with committed friends on a manufactured home on some land in a school district from which our kids would graduate and develop life-long friends.

Getting back into the only type of job I thought for which I had any skill, church work, was an uphill climb that tested my new-found movements in practicing humility. It was two steps forward and one step backward. I was happy to be alive and enjoying my family, yet the job was unsettling and unfulfilling. So I switched my measure of success from work to family. I attended school activities and learned how to be a dad who was present for his kids. This was part of the training ground of learning how to be humble.

Unearthing Buried Passion

Professionally, my passion for leadership and building a healthy culture was fueled, as I attended numerous workshops, seminars, and summits by thought leaders in these areas. As I devoured their books, I was enamored by their commitment to creating environments and experiences for people to succeed. As I scan my bookshelves today, the authors who have impacted me the most expounded on principles that shaped my thinking and that I teach to this day. It was more than an academic pursuit for me. I was learning how to be a transformational leader, not just the art but also the skill. Just to be clear, I was a Padawan (Jedi in training), with so much to learn.

One of the members of the congregation where I worked, the former trainer of the Detroit Red Wings and owner of a health club gave me a real gift. He knew I was passionate about leadership, and he asked if I would coach him in his business. I didn't know exactly what to do, but I felt comfortable in offering my opinion to him as a business leader. Challenge accepted!

His friend heard about it and asked if I would coach his work group through some leadership training. Why not? At this point, they asked me two questions I had never heard before: "What is the name of your company? And how much do you charge?" Uh…I thought I was doing this for free. I was given a taste of something that satisfied a much deeper appetite in me. Could this be something I really was drawn to? Could this be something that I wanted to do with my life? In any case, I started my business, Whatif Enterprises, LLC.

Ignoring My Emotional Life

Here's the kicker: just because I had gone through a traumatic health scare didn't mean that I got emotionally healthy or fully understood or implemented into my life the principles and practices of transformation. I virtually ignored most of my emotions and leaned heavily on my intellect and drive to learn. I showed up intellectually astute, not emotionally mature. It's all I knew. I didn't know then what I know now—that "Emotional health and spiritual maturity are inseparable. It is not possible to be spiritually mature while remaining emotionally immature." (*Emotionally Healthy Spirituality*) Today, you can take a test to measure your level of emotional and spiritual health. I can safely tell you that, at that time in my life, I would have scored "infant" in almost every category.

EMOTIONAL HEALTH AND SPIRITUAL MATURITY ARE INSEPARABLE.

I showed up as a cancer survivor and a family man, with newfound growing expertise in leadership and organizational health, yet it was plainly obvious to those closest to me that I was still insecure and seeking validation in all the wrong places. I liken my life to the Wizard in *The Wizard of Oz*—the Great and the Terrible. Near the end of the movie, when Dorothy and her companions secure the broom of the Wicked Witch of the West, as the Wizard ordered, they bring it to the Wizard. With bombastic pyrotechnics, he rejects the broom and tells them to go home. Dorothy's dog smells something awry. As Toto pulls back the curtain, the Wizard keeps talking and blowing smoke. Now, he is exposed. The truth is revealed. When Dorothy and her companions finally confront him, she blurts out the words, "Oh, you're a very bad man!" A fair response to such a display of fake power and prestige. The Wizard stumbles and fumbles, as he quietly shares authentic words from his heart, "Oh, no, my dear, I...I'm a very good man—I'm just a very bad Wizard."

That's me! I wanted to be a good man—seen as worthy, smart, successful, and more. I wanted to get this heart stuff right. I wanted to be a transformational person so that I could be a transformational leader. I read books from the Who's Who of transformation: Dallas Willard, Henri Nouwen, John Ortberg, John Eldredge, Richard Manning, Robert Quinn, and more (look them up on Amazon; I have read most of their books). The Appendix contains the *Top Ten Things I Learned.* What I didn't know is that I needed to deal with what was getting in the way: my false self grounded in EGO—wanting to be king of my kingdom.

My behavior professionally was also bleeding into my marriage and family life. We were not moving forward as a married couple, unless I got help, lots of help, real help. Essentially, the mandate was move out and don't come back, until you change.

My EGO had to die...again. I finally said, "Enough...I surrender!" I had to face the reality that I was a mess. This time the verses to my story were once again of great loss. I lost my career, my time as a pastor was permanently over. I lost my house and, most devastatingly, I completely alienated myself from my family. After years of putting on armor to protect myself, I had to be vulnerable. "Sucking it up" was no longer an option. The pain was too great to continue. Posing didn't work. Complying didn't work. Striving didn't work. There had to be another way.

The Path to Healing

With the help of wise friends, my patient wife and family, and a good therapist, I slowly gained clarity and inner healing. As painful as it was, it was so very, very good. Facing my deepest parts was the only path to healing.

I had never considered myself a hypocrite, yet when it came to living out that which was good and noble, all the fingers pointed back to me. I was the hypocrite! In fact, recognizing your own hypocrisy is the focal point of transformation. Take it from an academic in Actual Change Theory, Robert E. Quinn, "Over the years I have become focused on this notion of hypocrisy, and I have come to accept an unacceptable fact. I am a hypocrite. When I take this notion seriously, it makes changing myself much easier" (*Change the World*).

The one person who was instrumental in my life at that time and still today is my good friend, Tim Hogan. It is true that Tim is intelligent, creative, and compassionate. With degrees from Notre Dame and Fuller Theological Seminary, he is a Doctor of Psychology. He is an author and a speaker on embodied integration and is comfortable in intensive therapy sessions or in front of hundreds of people. More importantly for me, Tim is one of the few people whom I trust with the depth of my story and he trusts me with his.

What I mean by that is that our story is so important, so sacred, that we can trust only a small group of people with the depth of it. They are the only ones who can and should handle it. Even as I write this book, you are not getting the depths of my story. I am vulnerable, but there are layers of pain and celebration that I dare not share with you. You haven't journeyed with me closely enough to handle the sacredness of it.

Believe me, as a people pleaser who overshares, that was a tough lesson to learn. I consistently overshared out of shame, hoping that if I told people a lot, they would like me. This backfires every time, and it is not satisfying for the sharer or the listener of the story. Therefore, I encourage people to have three levels of story depending on the depth of the relationship. Level One: the five-minute story that you share for those with whom you may work or for those who are first coming into your acquaintance. Level Two: the thirty-minute story that you share with those with whom you want to develop a more vulnerable relationship. Level Three: the two-hour story that you share with your small circle of trusted folks.

Not Doing Life Alone

Tim and I have been friends for over two decades, the only person, besides my wife, who has been in a relationship with me that long. He has seen me at my best and has witnessed me at my worst, including being at the brunt of some selfish decisions, where I lied directly to his face. In most worlds, that would sever any relationship and be chalked up as permanent betrayal. In Tim's world, it meant hurt and, more important, love, a level of unconditional love that I didn't deserve. And that is the point. Tim's gift of grace for me is not earned; it's given. His gift of love for me is not measured; it's abundant.

From our personality, gifts, looks, family traditions, and church backgrounds, we couldn't be more different. Yet we grew up as two little boys who longed to be noticed and loved, who married women who loved us despite who we are, who grew up as men who tried to figure out life on our own and to get our validation from other people. Though our paths were different, the journey was the same. Henri Nouwen's words sum up our quest:

> "Over the years, I have come to realize that the greatest trap in our life is not success, popularity, or power, but self-rejection. Success, popularity, and power can indeed present a great temptation, but their seductive quality often comes from the way they are part of the much larger temptation to self-rejection. When we have come to believe in the voices that call us worthless and unlovable, then success, popularity, and power are easily perceived as attractive solutions. The real trap, however, is self-rejection. As soon as someone accuses me or criticizes me, as soon as I am rejected, left alone, or abandoned, I find myself thinking, 'Well, that proves once again that I am a nobody. ... [My dark side says,] I am no good... I deserve to be pushed aside, forgotten, rejected, and abandoned. Self-rejection is the greatest enemy of the spiritual life because it contradicts the sacred voice that calls us the Beloved.' Being the Beloved constitutes the core truth of our existence" (*Life of the Beloved*).

There you have it. Either I choose to get my validation from other people, or I lean into the reality that I am beloved.

It's good to have people affirm me. They can certainly disagree with me or criticize me. But it doesn't change my identity. When Tim and I go off the rails and forget this truth, we remind each other to get back on track. When our "dark-side" voice gets loud or screams obnoxiously, we remind each other of the truth. In fact, Tim taught me the simple rhythm for how to handle the "dark side," which some would refer to as "the inner critic." This is the oft-repeated mantra, sometimes in my head and sometimes out loud, "There you are [my friend]; I see you; I hear you. You are not the truth, and I am moving forward in the truth of who I really am…broken and beloved." I would like to tell you that it works every time. Not only would I like to tell you that it works every time; I will also tell you that it works every time. It works—EVERY TIME!

Getting Professional Help

I am also grateful for the season I spent with Jackie, my therapist. Just to be clear, I was a horrible client. To protect myself, I put up roadblocks to deter her. They didn't work. She was a strong woman, with a keen "bullshit meter." She had worked in the prison system and knew how to handle insecure men who abused their power. Besides her tenacious spirit, the best gift she gave me was time, lots of time. Because it was early in her practice and because she believed that healing meant spending time with clients, most of my sessions lasted from two to four hours, twice a week. You read that correctly.

Here are some of her words that I remember. I am fondly calling it: *Five Lessons from My Therapist*

1. Quit reading books, and explore you. You may be well-read on most subjects in your area of expertise, yet you have no clue about your own voice.

2. Get an effective emotional vocabulary. Here is a feeling wheel; let's learn to examine how you really feel.

3. Get healed, and others will experience the change, because you are different. Don't try to win people (your family) back with your words. They will know when you have changed; they will experience a different you, because you will be okay with who you are.

4. WHO you are matters more than WHAT you do…and, by the way, WHO are you?

5. You will be stronger, now that you are broken. [As she took a taper candle in her hands and crushed it, she lit the candle and let the wax drip.] This broken candle will be stronger, now that it is broken.

It will not come as surprise that this experience also healed and transformed the way I view and treat women. I began to see the dignity, depth and power of women. I began to experience their feminine energy as a gift. I learned not to be dependent on women to validate me, thereby being codependent or afraid of them at some deep level. I learned I didn't have to pose or pretend to be confident. I learned to make the choice to join them in the human experience of life; co-equally living out our uniqueness. Today, I have the privilege of knowing hundreds of women who I respect and honor, both professionally and personally. With each one I can be my authentic self.

I also have wonderful relationships with the women in my immediate family. My wife, Deb, has found her voice, and she is a strong, gracious woman with a mature, fun-loving presence. I have two strong daughters and a daughter-in-law that I respect and admire. They don't need an unhealed, passive-aggressive male who chooses to emotionally ignore them. They simply want me to show up as me. Yes, they tolerate my goofiness and confront my mistakes and misconceptions, and whenever they see me, they give me a genuine hug and tell me they love me. At times, they will joke about the "old Mark" and tell me how happy they are with the "new Mark"—even calling me "Rafiki." In fact, a recent Christmas gift was a canvas with pictures of each of my grandchildren with me, with the words in the center that Rafiki spoke to Simba (*The Lion King*), "Look inside yourself. You are more than what you have become." I am so grateful… It was a challenging road to get here.

Living Life While Healing

To survive financially, I tended bar, cleaned toilets, and did a setup at a conference center. My fellow employees didn't care about my degree, my knowledge, or my past career. They simply wanted me to show up: to do my job and not to be an asshole. Another path to healing. When I wasn't working, the rest of my time was spent learning about me. Separated from my family, I had lots of time to think, cry, weep, grieve, learn, and eventually accept me. The only way to change was from the inside out.

Think about what you have heard or read from people reflecting on what it was like going through a challenging time. The type of hardship doesn't matter. The common thread is that it often brought them to a dark place. St. John of the Cross, a sixteenth-century Spanish mystic and poet referred to it as the "dark night of the soul." In the poem by that title, he expresses life's challenges in the context of leading us back to the divine.

It is true; as I came out of it, there was a transformation, a new perspective. Without regret, they say, "These dark places are the best things that could have happened to me." I join them.

Five Lessons from the Dark Days (Years)

1. People don't care about how much you know; they want to know if you genuinely care about them.

2. All people matter! There are wonderful life lessons to learn from all people, regardless of their education, sexual orientation, skin color, and more.

3. You don't have to be an expert to be appreciated.

4. Serve others with a servant's heart.

5. Be faithful and fully show up, no matter what!

And because life fits the perfect crescendo and resolution of a song, as I was on the path to transformation, making real changes and learning about WHO I was, another verse was added to my Good Ole' Country western tune. Ten years to the date of my initial bout with cancer and other losses, life proved that it is messy, complicated, and unexpected.

Reprise

A man schemed his way into our lives.

He took advantage of our new beginning by making promises of a joint business endeavor.

We were one of five families that entrusted him with tens of thousands of dollars.

He lied, cheated, manipulated, and coerced at every level.

In the end, just our family was scammed out of $70K,

Losing our savings,

Keeping us in debt for the next seven years.

Chorus

I began to realize that my life was a gift,

And that, maybe, just maybe,

> *Love was the key,*

And that life wasn't all about me.

My wife and children loved me deeply, and we grew close.

Humility was happening without my effort.

Breathe and Pause

How might you be transmitting pain to others?

What hypocrisy might you need to face?

What would it mean if you experienced some type of EGO "death" to transformation?

Who are the people that are instrumental in supporting your transformation?

The most extraordinary people in the world today don't have a career. They have a mission. –VISHEN LAKHIANI

What will happen when we focus on what is right with people rather than fixating on what is wrong with them.
–DONALD O CLIFTON

CHAPTER 7

Finding Your Sweet Spot

After only a few months of bartending and cleaning toilets at the conference center the owners, who knew my passion for leadership and organizational health, offered me a job as general manager. By this time, I was an avid believer in the principles of Patrick Lencioni and The Table Group (*The Four Obsessions of an Extraordinary Executive: A Leadership Fable* and *The Five Dysfunctions of a Team: A Leadership Fable*). Without other options on the horizon, I was immersed in business life, while being given the opportunity to practice my principles of building a healthy culture and a personal development in the brutally earthy food-service industry. I learned so much.

The managing owner of the conference center was a real gift to me. Jim Harkema was a lettered athlete, who had spent his career as football coach at Grand Valley State University and Eastern Michigan University. He knew how to win, and, more important, he understood people and how to inspire them; he was a true transformational leader. It was a thrill for me to hear his stories and insights about college football. He was a huge supporter of my work on personal and professional development. We exchanged many ideas and conversed about principles from books we were reading.

One principle I learned from Jim shifted the tectonic plates in my mind. I still remember the time when I first heard him say, "I believe in abundance mentality. The more I help others succeed, the better it is for everyone." What…abundance mentality? I had no idea what it was and what it meant. So much of our culture, me included, seems to be built on a scarcity mentality—believing there is a lack of life and opportunities. An abundance mentality, a term coined by Stephen Covey is "a concept in which a person believes there are enough resources and successes to share with others" (*The Seven Habits of a Highly Effective Person*). I watched Jim exude happiness, despite the circumstances; take advantage of opportunities; engage with people; celebrate others' accomplishments; and have a sense of security in his endeavors. He wanted my success, and, in turn, I wanted his success.

Steps Out of a Scarcity Mentality

1. Recognize the truth of your scarcity mentality. You believe that there is a lack in life; everyone "has," and you do not "have." You believe that you just stumble into opportunities and that you have no choice in matters. Therefore, you live with limitations, and negativity becomes your modus operandi.

2. Choose to believe differently. Begin to focus your mind and attention toward people and circumstances that are good, beautiful, and beneficial.

3. Be grateful. Begin a gratitude journal, and write down three new things (such as people, circumstances, relationships, and opportunities) every day for which you are grateful. Start speaking words of appreciation and gratefulness. The very act of speaking builds a habit.

4. Learn from people with an abundance mentality. Hang out with them; study them. Notice their mind-set, their conversation, their approach, their vibe, and more.

5. Create "win-win" situations with every opportunity. Look for ways to serve others, and genuinely seek to meet potential needs they might express.

6. Keep practicing. There will be moments when you will slip back into the dark hole of thinking scarcely. When you do, notice it. Ask yourself how you got there. And then start back at #1. Welcome to the journey of training.

Transformational Opportunities

Are you living in truth? I found that when my life was not around building my kingdom, but around serving others, amazing things could happen. There were fantastic opportunities to love people, to offer them dignity, and to create a safe working environment. Not only were Deb's and my life transforming (she worked there, as well); so also were the lives of many others.

For lack of a better analogy, I was starting to find my own voice. I was living the truth of my story and not the fables—untruths—I let others write for me. Ironically, I had spent my lifetime talking. For over two decades, I was expected to talk well and get paid for it. However, that did not mean that I had found my own voice. In the healing process, I learned that I needed to fight for things that are good and beneficial. In this season of my life, I needed to fight for me. Rather than being an outward battle of words, it would be an internal battle of what is true about me. Challenge accepted!

In the seminal leadership book, *Good to Great,* Jim Collins rocked the business world with his "three questions around the Hedgehog concept: 1) What are you deeply passionate about? 2) To what can you aspire to be the best in the world? 3) What drives your economic engine?" His concept has stood the test of time as three questions that organizations must answer with utmost clarity. However, I never heard people talk about this short paragraph in the book,

> "To quickly grasp the three circles, consider the following personal analogy. Suppose you were able to construct a work life that meets the following three tests. First, you are doing work for which you have a genetic or God-given talent…Second, you are well paid for doing what you do…Third, you are doing work you are passionate about and absolutely love to do, enjoying the actual process for its own sake."

I couldn't believe me ears. I wanted that type of clarity around those three questions. When I heard Collins speak at a conference, he made the same personal application. I was hooked. I began a quest much like that of the Holy Grail so that I could confidently answer those questions. My quest had a goal.

I went onto the Franklin Covey website and recall reading

that Covey and his colleagues had a process to find your mission statement within five minutes. No way! You can't find your personal mission in five minutes. I had spent fifty years trying to find my voice; there is no way you can discover it that quickly. As a *move against,* I went to work trying to figure the mission of my life. It didn't take long for me to realize that there were other questions to ask and answer first. Questions such as the following: What are my core values? What is my purpose? What are my unique talents? How do I want to show up to the world—my mission?

The research began on the ways for me to answer those questions. My background in a writing curriculum and love for learning inspired me to dig deeply into a process to answer those questions. Uncovering my purpose, core values, talents, and mission was a very intentional process. It involved questioning, probing, journaling, and self-reflection. Obstacles, many of which had been self-imposed and that had blocked me in the past, needed to be faced. It demanded a level of self-awareness that I was learning to value and practice.

First, I had to become a student of myself. An essential part of this quest was understanding the principles and practice of emotional intelligence. As I began to develop an effective emotional vocabulary, I studied in earnest the work of Daniel Goleman. His article, "What Makes a Leader" (*Harvard Business Review,* November–December 1998) and subsequent books, *Emotional Intelligence* and *Primal Leadership,* were my guides on the quest. His premise was that the best leaders had one thing in common: emotional intelligence. He went so far as to say that it was "twice as important as technical skills and IQ!" In my academic career and parochial culture, the only thing that mattered or was celebrated was IQ and technical skill. Emotional intelligence held no weight. Passion was dismissed as futile. It was as if Goleman's writing were a love letter to my dried-up and desperate spirit. Not only did my "head" matter, but so did my "heart." Transformational leaders lead from both head and heart, and the essential practice is self-awareness and self-management.

Second, I needed to be clear on the principles that keep me grounded. I knew what it meant to veer off course; moving forward, I needed to be clear about my core values. The process of uncovering them and eventually articulating them was and is the foundation for how I live my life. They shape my attitude and guide my behavior. They provide focus when I am unclear. They are unbending when I want to waver. Knowing your personal core values is not an option for living a transformational life; knowing them is a necessity.

> KNOWING YOUR PERSONAL CORE VALUES IS NOT AN OPTION FOR LIVING A TRANSFORMATIONAL LIFE; KNOWING THEM IS A NECESSITY.

Third, the more I learned about myself, the more I realized that while my core values would remain the same, I would be ever changing and growing. I needed to embrace the process of learning about the ways my transformation would impact others.

Given the green light to build a culture as general manager, I focused on building transformational leaders—people of influence, no matter their role on the org chart.

I worked tirelessly to put together a makeshift way to identify my core values and to uncover my purpose. But I still needed the "how" answers: How will I fulfill my purpose? What is my mission? What are my answers to the Hedgehog Circle questions?

First, Break All the Rules (Buckingham and Coffman) was my introduction to a new way of managing people in a way that bucked conventional wisdom. At the same time, a friend recommended *Now, Discover Your Strengths* (Buckingham). It immediately made sense to me and seemed like such a practical way to find one's "fit." I was hooked.

True to my nature, which is to dive into something that interests me, I read *StrengthsFinder 2.0* (Rath), took the Strengths Assessment, and immersed myself in the strengths-based philosophy. While I won't repeat the insights and meaning of this concept in its entirety, it's important to my story to share my top five Talent Themes. They are: WOO, MAXIMIZER, RELATOR, EMPATHY, CONNECTEDNESS.

Like a significant number of people who see their talent themes for the first time, I was not pleased with my "top five." First, they felt "soft." After all, how could I be a successful business coach with talents that, from my perspective, could not impact the bottom line? Second, I had been told since I was a young boy that I had the power to WOO (Win Over Others). It may have been a well-intended compliment, but I had recoded those messages to hear that I was more of a cheerleader than an intellectual giant. Based on my past; this felt somehow inferior.

After the initial distain, I stepped back and took a deep dive into learning about talents. The truth was that these messages were right on. I also noted that each time I attempted to fix my weaknesses, it backfired. These efforts to change those parts of myself, ended in frustration, embarrassment, and failure.

I became convinced that Donald Clifton, the founder of the strength's movement, was right; "playing to strengths" would be my mantra.

I would spend more time and energy developing my gifts and leveraging my natural talents. I would take a cue from athletics: do what you do best.

Many of the missing pieces of the puzzle toward personal growth and success became clearer over the next couple of years.

I learned about myself: what thoughts, feelings, and actions inspired me and what activities I, quite frankly, loathed. This awareness was a game changer.

Fourth, I noticed things that excited me, that drove me, and what I wanted to do more of. I enjoyed building a staff of satisfied and productive employees: leading people was about focusing on individuals' strengths and helping them learn to manage weaknesses, not fix them. I implemented the vision of moving people into roles where they could "play to their strengths." When they played to their strengths, they were invigorated, learned more, and were the most creative.

I had an insatiable need to learn more about strengths by adding *StrengthsQuest* (Clifton and Anderson) to my repertoire.

Yet I wanted still more…I wanted some type of training. I called Gallup in 2007, ready to sign up for any training Gallup's managers offered. I hung up the phone, disappointed that their focus at that time was on Fortune 500 companies. I was on my own in my journey to learn the most I could about my new-found passion for strengths. My goal was to become a strength's expert. I use the word "expert" more to convey the depth of my intentionality as I study. My journey is circuitous, at best.

In my spare time, I was still working as a general manager, and I devoured any information I could about strengths: *Go, Put Your Strengths to Work* (Buckingham), Harvard Business Review articles, blogs. And I had dozens of conversations on such topics as strengths. In my professional life, I practiced, through trial and error, how to lead, to manage, and to train people with my best understanding of the strengths-based philosophy. I was both gaining real-life experience and refining ideas and practices as I worked with my employees.

What started out as a personal exercise in self-discovery was slowly becoming a tool that maybe, just maybe, might benefit others in their own journey. Over time, I put the pieces together as part of the first version of what is now called MissionBuilder,™ which was designed to help others walk through the same steps to find, articulate and own their core values, purpose, and mission.

Check out www.RecalibrateYou.com, a uniquely designed process to optimize your life around clarity, purpose, and action.

Breathe and Pause

What are positive principles you have learned from others?

How would you answer the Hedgehog Concept questions?

Are you doing work for which you have a genetic or God-given talent?

Are you getting paid for doing what you do?

Are you doing work you are passionate about and absolutely love to do, enjoying the actual process for its own sake?

If you want help with these questions, consider embarking on the six-month journey of MissionBuilder.™ www.recalibrateyou.com

*The first and most important choice a leader
makes is the choice to serve, without which one's capacity
to lead is severely limited.* –ROBERT GREENLEAF

Life's most urgent question is, "What are you doing for others?"
–MARTIN LUTHER KING JR.

CHAPTER 8

Living Out of Mission

My first "gig" in coaching around strengths occurred when Tim Hogan Psy.D. hired me to help him work through MissionBuilder.™ This experience afforded me the opportunity to synthesize my learnings, test hypotheses, and really consider the process I would use to share this with someone else. I already knew how to write curriculum; it was a matter of becoming a subject-matter expert.

Within a year, Tim invited me to share MissionBuilder™ with the staff at his counseling center in Metro-Detroit. A few months later, the former director, who was then running a men's ministry, invited me to do MissionBuilder™ with his group of twenty-five men. Initially I declined, because I had designed MissionBuilder™ for individual coaching, not larger groups. He insisted. I was a bit apprehensive, as I drove to what we in Metro-Detroit call the East Side for my group session. The men were open, engaged, and inspired. MissionBuilder™ resonated with this group of men.

In that group were three "C-Level" business leaders who were interested in hiring me to work with their teams. A major shift started to happen that day, both for me and for them. I went from being a teacher to a content expert. I went from giving them a lesson on strengths and missions to being a resource that would help their businesses. This was my first foray into becoming a coach, and eventually a trusted advisor. I left that day feeling like it was a huge step for me. While it was, I didn't realize that my foray was not going to be a straight and direct one. My journey to coach would take much longer than I wanted or intended, with pauses, fits, starts, and many detours.

One of the leaders wanted MissionBuilder,™ but the other two wanted training only in strengths. Shortsighted, I told them that strengths was only a part of the MissionBuilder™ process and that it all needed to be included. After they told me it was strengths or nothing, I relented and started developing new training tools for their leadership teams around strengths, thereby launching my strengths teaching and my strengths coaching. Within weeks, I was training senior leaders in the business world, a whole new experience for me, nerve-racking and exhilarating.

Once people were introduced to their talent themes, my role as teacher-trainer was to provide the right environment and trusted processes to help them integrate strengths into their current professional and personal life. This meant increasing my portfolio of implementation tools and individual coaching sessions. Parenthetically, one of the teams included individual coaching sessions. Little did I know that this approach would be a staple for my work going forward.

Learning Lessons in Every Circumstance

All this was happening while I served as general manager of a conference center, with a niche to host high-end weddings and conferences for groups numbering from 25 to 225. Have you ever had to close a bar at the end of wedding reception after people have been drinking free alcohol for five hours? It was one thing to talk to people in the lobby after a Sunday service and listen to the stories or sit in congregational meetings, where well-meaning volunteer committee members were paralyzed in making decisions. It's quite another thing to hold off a well-lubed drunk who is swearing at you, "I have to have another drink, or the whole event will be ruined. You $^&#!" That was the rule, not the exception. We hosted approximately twenty-five weddings a year: marketing, selling, planning, preparing, prepping, providing, and cleaning up.

As bizarre as the schedule was and as colorful as the clientele could be, I grew to love the unique situation and the people that I worked with. Those people and experiences left indelible impressions on my leadership.

Max was a server in a five-star restaurant and gave up his job to be a bartender during the Superbowl in Detroit, to tend bar and make $10K for the week. He was smooth and aloof but could handle table after table with excellence.

The protocol after every wedding was that every server and support staff would stay until about 2:00 a.m. to clean up and set up for Monday's events. Just after the wedding ended and the last drunken guests stumbled out the door, I would host a winding-down meeting to debrief the people with whom I worked and to divvy out assignments to them. On Max's first night, I gave him and myself the assignment to clean the bathrooms. Max said quietly, "I don't do f*%@n bathrooms!" I took a deep breath and said, "Okay; then you can just watch me." That's exactly what he did. He didn't lift a finger to help me for over an hour. The next Saturday evening, I gave Max and myself the same assignment. He had the same response. However, this time, he picked up a rag and cleaned the mirrors for the last five minutes. The third week, I gave Max and myself the same assignment. This time, in front of everyone, Max stated, "I got them, Mark. You don't have to help me." Everyone was stunned and inquired about his change of heart. "If the general manager can clean the bathrooms, so can I."

Remember: I am a *move against.* My inclination was to rip Max a new one at his first response. Yet I was going through the fire of transfor-

I WAS GOING THROUGH THE FIRE OF TRANSFORMATION.

mation. I was beginning to understand that a transactional person was EGO-centric and, in my case, demanding and combative. I had started to practice the positive aspects of a *move against.* What if I would fight for what is right? What if I could stand on principle and just let Max see that choosing to serve is the higher road? What if I led as a transformational leader?

I have fond memories of so many people who worked for me. Each one had a story. Each one was longing for dignity. I would hear things like the following:

"This is safest space for me right now. My home isn't safe. My

family isn't safe. This is where I have the most peace."

"I was doing tricks just to make ends meet, before I started working here. I have been told I am nothing but a worthless asshole my whole life. Do you really mean it when you say, 'I am beloved'?"

"Before I came to work here, I was in a dead-end job, with no purpose and no hope for the future. Now I am gaining self-esteem, as what I do here matters; you saw worth in me."

"My Sunday mornings when my family was at church was five hours of porn and cocaine. Now it's a morning coffee, reading the paper, and conversing with my wife."

"So the reason why the Italians call the pope "papa" is that he is their spiritual dad. Well, then, Mark, I guess that makes you my papa."

I am holding back the tears as I write this. I had spent years standing in front of people, teaching truths that I had hoped would change lives, yet I had lost myself. And, now, I am coming out of a time of confusion and am simply loving people and offering them dignity. Their responses of gratitude are about working in a transformative environment.

Breathe and Pause

What do you do in the face of challenges?

When someone antagonizes you, what is your reaction? How does that work for you?

What would it mean for you to simply show up and "be" yourself at work?

I think so many times in our society we focus so much on just the end result; when we finally reach that point, we realize that was never the true goal. –Apolo Ohno

Our greatest successes in life often come through helping others to succeed, and without question, when you focus on helping others succeed your eventual payoff will always be far greater than your investment. –Amy Rees Anderson

CHAPTER 9

Accepting Help

The conference center closed in 2009 thanks to mix of Michigan's horrible economy and bad ownership decisions. Deb had spent years as an event planner and was invited to work for the executive chef. He opened his own business and had provided all food and service to Cleary University, which was just a few miles from our home. He was so grateful for my informal coaching when we worked together and asked me to be his first official client. It was time for me to dedicate all my time to building my coaching practice.

I approached this building season like any achiever: reading, researching, networking, and seeking out other people like me, from whom I might learn.

I filled out my LinkedIn profile and had eight contacts. I found a female executive coach on the West coast who had eighty-eight contacts. So I emailed her to connect. To my chagrin, her response was that she didn't know me; however, if I spent some time with her on the phone, she might consider it. What? Who does that? On a snowy February afternoon, I was on a phone with a woman I had never met, who was asking me questions about what I liked to do. After thirty minutes, her words were simple and direct: "You have a lot to offer. Join at least three different LinkedIn groups that align with your expertise. Post questions. Respond to others so that you are seen as a subject-matter expert. And, by the way, I am going to be watching on LinkedIn to see if you do this." Challenge accepted!

I showed up on LinkedIn with a vengeance. I joined two groups that catapulted me into new relationships and a circle of networking I could never have imagined.

In a *StrengthsFinder, I Know My Strengths* group, I met people in the strengths movement who are passionate, intelligent, humble, and gifted. Their willingness to encourage others and share their experience is unparalleled. Each of us ventured out on our own, and the group provided us a space to share our passion for organizational development, with a love for strengths. Deedra was passionate about strengths, and since she lived in southeast Michigan, we met regularly for conversations and mutual sharing. It is safe to say she was my first coach. She shared all her learning and encouraged me to follow my passion to help people maximize their strengths.

The second group was *The Five Dysfunctions* group, where I started a new discussion post with, "Lencioni's new book is out, *Getting Naked*; have you read it? Is it worth it?" Within three days, people from all the world were commenting on it. One guy lived only twenty miles from my house and asked if we could get together for coffee. I didn't know then that Jim was the former CEO of a $1.4 billion company, which had given him a platform to speak to hundreds of executives each year around the world, on the importance of building organizations that were both "smart and healthy." And he knew Patrick Lencioni. This former army officer's first words to me were, "Who are you and why in the hell don't I know you?" I was stunned. I was a schmuck who was trying to figure out how to help people and who wanted to practice the principles of Lencioni, and Jim knew him! Yikes! Jim was used to his peers, those who liked to talk about the importance of healthy teams but seemed stuck to have found someone who actually liked to do the work of helping executives build them. He was shocked that this was what I liked to do. I assured him that I had been prepared for this after years of counseling, funerals, weddings, and church meetings.

He wanted me to meet Donna. It was a warm summer afternoon when her schedule was cleared to meet me. I didn't know then that Donna had spent years coaching executives who are the Who's Who of large companies on the west side of Michigan. I asked Donna how she stayed grounded as a coach. She reflected on a directive from her spiritual advisor to spend an extended time in retreat with God. She asked me, and I shared with her my regular practice of prayer, mediation, reading, and journaling. She retorted, "You intrigue me. Do you speak?" Of course, I had, but it had been years since an official speaking gig. "On what topic?" Here was my opportunity to put it out there: transformational leadership. Without hesitation, she told me that she wanted to put me in front of a group of VP and C-level leaders so that I could lead a discussion on transformational leadership. Our bond strengthened around transformational leadership, as it complimented her work with vision and execution. Her strategic talents helped me develop practical tools in integrating strengths.

A few weeks later, I was prepared to lead a three-hour interactive workshop on a topic that was not only dear to my heart but also life changing. I showed up more nervous than I had ever been. Preaching and teaching to a thousand people was stimulating. This was terrifying. So I dug up as much courage as I could and showed up. After three hours, the audience asked if I could stay the day and continue to lead the discussion.

So I dug up as much courage as I could and showed up.

Two months later, Donna put me in front of two different groups of CEOs, presidents, and business owners to lead the same workshop. A couple of weeks later, she and Jim invited me to a peer group to explain my process of *Strengths Training* and MissionBuilder.™

Apparently, I was the only coach whom the peer group members interviewed who had a process. They invited me to join their peer group and would begin to recommend me to their clients as a partner with an expertise in *Strengths Training* and building healthy teams.

Making It Happen versus Letting It Happen

The worst thing we can do is try to push things to happen in our timeline. I had learned the hard way that doesn't work. So as all of this came about, I didn't orchestrate any of it. I spent my efforts staying grounded, working on my interior world, and making sure that whatever process I offered people would bring value. Again, I had spent most of my life striving to make things happen, hoping that I would do enough to be validated and to be seen as being enough.

What I was learning were two very important principles. First, good people want to help you succeed. One motivational speaker put it this way, "Successful people are always looking for opportunities to help others. Unsuccessful people are always asking, 'What's in it for me?'" I had spent too many years asking the selfish question. Now I was rubbing shoulders with people who believed the opposite. Second, by just being myself, being clear about WHO I am and WHAT I do, I could bring my best self to others. I could offer both my mind and my heart, and that would be enough. As broken and beloved, I am enough. Let the results happen.

It was a whole new way of showing up. I put to memory the following quotation from Henri Nouwen, Dutch Catholic priest and spiritual writer (*Life of the Beloved*): "Our life itself is the greatest gift to give—something we constantly forget. The real question is not 'What can we offer others?' but 'Who can we be for each other?' The greatest gift I have to offer is my own joy of living, my own inner peace, my own silence and solitude, my own sense of well-being."

Breathe and Pause

Who are the people you have asked for help? What did you experience?

Who are the people you could offer your help to, as you help them become successful?

Each day holds a surprise. But only if we expect it can we see, feel, or hear it when it comes to us. Let's not be afraid to receive each day's surprise, whether it comes to us as sorrow or joy. It will open up a new place in our hearts, a place where we can welcome new friends and celebrate more fully our shared humanity. –HENRI NOUWEN

CHAPTER 10

Open to Surprises

"I started Whatif Enterprises, LLC—Chauffer Division." That was the joke with my family when I came home from a coaching appointment and they asked me what was new today.

As I sat at the kitchen table of one of my clients waiting for my personal coaching session, I was killing time talking with her husband. He embarrassingly asked me if I knew anyone who could drive him around for a few months, as he made sales calls. He had lost his license and needed a chauffeur for a few months. He would pay $10.00 per hour. For a few seconds, I was thinking of names of people, because this time was before Uber; then I got the nudge that I should be the driver. Here's the internal dialog that probably took five seconds but seemed like a long conversation with myself. "We are tight on cash right now, as we wait for clients. Nope! I am not going to chauffer. You have got to be kidding me? I have clients to coach and teams to build. This is ridiculous. I didn't get this far in my life to become a driver." Before I knew it, I agreed, and my new gig started.

A few days later, I got into his minivan, and we headed to the jail for him to give a urine sample. As he walked out the door, he looked different than most of the people for many reasons, one of which was his expensive suit. When he got into the car, I said, "That has to be hard for you…very humbling!" He began to cry. And then he directed me to the nearest Coney Island, where we talked. We spent the rest of the day in deep conversation as I drove; I asked questions and listened. Eight hours later, he said, "You know, Mark, you were not only my driver today; you were also my coach. I am paying you to drive. I'm also going to pay you to be my coach. Let's do this again next time." I drove home, humbled and grateful. I simply showed up for this man, and that was enough. With tears, I showed my wife the $80 for driving and the $120 for coaching that day. Whew! She cried with me.

A few months later, I had a conversation with the dean of students at Cleary University, during which time, he asked if I would be interested in being an adjunct instructor. I had the time; we needed the money; it would look good on my résumé; and I enjoyed teaching. This was a pleasant surprise. I learned from the students as much as I was teaching them. For the next two years, I taught classes that focused in three separate disciplines:

Management: Leadership & Teams / Behavior of Organizations

Entrepreneurship: Creativity & Innovation

Event and Meeting Management: Event Food & Beverage Management

How are you invited to show up each day? If you are like me, you have preconceived ideas of what your day might be like and what you want to accomplish. That is a good thing. I wonder, though, what it would be like to have enough space in your day for the surprises. The moment when a coworker needs a couple of extra minutes of your attention, so you put the phone down or turn away from your computer to listen. The moment as you walk out the door for lunch, and someone asks you for a minute, and he or she just wants someone to listen to a pain or a hurt. The moment when you get home, and your spouse seems a bit frenzied from the day and, instead of diving into the next task, you look at your spouse long enough to notice what is needed, a word of encouragement or maybe a long, silent hug.

> I WONDER, THOUGH, WHAT IT WOULD BE LIKE TO HAVE ENOUGH SPACE IN YOUR DAY FOR THE SURPRISES.

People notice how we show up. If we show up ready to welcome the surprise conversations, the surprise encounters, the surprise "whatever," it may be the most meaningful gift they receive that day.

Breathe and Pause

What would it mean for you to be open to the surprises that come your way?

At times our own light goes out and is rekindled by a spark from another person. Each of us has cause to think with deep gratitude of those who have lighted the flame within us.
–ALBERT SCHWEITZER

Gratitude changes the pangs of memory into a tranquil joy.
–DIETRICH BONHOEFFER

CHAPTER 11

Learning the Gift of Gratitude

The more I studied personal development and leadership, the more I heard the principle that other people want to help you and to contribute whatever they can to your success. The more I tested the premise, the more I found it to be true. In fact, it's now my modus operandi.

I have already mentioned a few people who were more than happy to invest in my future success. Here are a few more. While these specific people are important to me, my hope is that you, as you read this, are inspired to be grateful for the people in your life and to be open to look for character traits in others that are worth cultivating.

Grateful for Others

It was so good to reconnect with my second cousin and friend, Dr. John Johnson, director at Living Hope Christian Counseling. We found out that we had been going through a similar journey, from transactional to transformational thinking and living. As someone who wants to see people reach their potential, he wanted to introduce his friends and key influencers to me and my workshop on Strengths. That first workshop in a room in a church in DePere, Wisconsin, led to many friendships and business relationships. It also was the genesis of an extensive leadership training program at a large church called Transformational Discipleship.

The eighteen-month program has six modules (quarters), and each quarter begins with a two-day retreat. Participants are screened and, upon approval of their applications, are assigned a coach and an accountability partner and become part of a book-discussion group (a new book is assigned each quarter). The three-fold emphasis of the program is:

1. Being Grounded: Both Spiritually and Emotionally

2. Living with Purpose

3. Living Out Your Unique Calling

The intentionality of the process allows the participants to do a deep dive into each discipline. As of this writing, one hundred people have participated. I could fill another chapter of the testimonies of lives who have been changed. It is truly transformational.

Chris Elias was part of a peer group of Trusted Advisors, with Jim and Donna. During a short walk to lunch, Chris succinctly summed up what would be the next few years of my life, "You have a great process. It's going to take three-to-five years to build your business." These words were both affirming and alarming at the same time. Growing up in the church world, I had no idea about the span of time it would take to build a business. Chris, on the other hand, was a member of the Elias family and the second generation to build the international organization of Elias Brothers Big Boy. He worked his way through the company, understood national and internal business, and sat in the executive chair for years, before the business was sold. His focus now was helping medium-to-large organizations develop the right strategy and implement a plan of execution that worked. Chris also has a keen awareness that the implementation of the plan depends on the right people being on the right seats of the bus and creating the right culture. Chris is brilliant, articulate, has a deep well of business knowledge, and can think on his feet with such lightning speed you would think you have just accessed the hard drive of a supercomputer.

At first, he would bring me in for individual coaching opportunities. Many of them were very challenging. With each opportunity, Chris and I would converse. Chris approached me with a vision—another one of his amazing gifts: what if we combine his work with strategy and execution, along with my work in people development. After all, he shared that so much of the challenges his clients had were on the people side of business. After years of talking and dreaming, we shared our company's core values. They were almost an exact match. It was the genesis of something new.

Chris introduced me to his coach, Ross Slater, a wise strategic thinker with amazing facilitation talents and an all-around nice guy whom he had known for years. After the proper vetting, Ross was now our coach. Knowing that so many business partnerships start out with good intentions and eventually implode, Ross put us through the paces. The more serious we became, the more Ross would push into things. His final encouragement—okay, prescriptive demand—was to work on a partnership charter. Think of a prenup for business partners. For months, Chris and I pounded through topic after topic that ended up being a forty-page document covering such topics as our stories, our hopes, our dreams, our fears, our strengths, our weaknesses, our talents, and our personalities. While we knew we couldn't cover every topic, we were going to do our due diligence. Since both Chris and I had been burned in previous business relationships, we were going to be extra careful about this one. Eventually, we agreed, and Nexecute, LLC was formed. Our focus tag line is SMARTER. FASTER. STRONGER. If the right plan is executed by the right people in the right culture, it will optimize your results.

Another person added to my list of people for whom I am grateful is Pete Emhoff. He has a great story and a journey of transformation. His passion is to help men break free from the stuff (think agreements) that hold them down and to invite them to live in freedom. I had met Pete when I was still serving as a pastor but, throughout my challenging years, we lost touch. As my head cleared, I saw Pete on LinkedIn (go figure) and reached out to connect. We shared our stories over a long lunch and decided to keep in touch.

I was intrigued by Pete's passion for helping men and for offering what he called "community and brothers." Honestly, those were trigger words for me. Any community or brotherhood I was a part of for decades wasn't psychologically or emotionally safe. What mattered most was being right. If anyone would say something that was outside of the right lingo or accepted dogma, their intentions and beliefs would be challenged. Their very loyalty to the group was questioned and the focus became on sussing out whether or not that person belonged. When Pete and his "brothers" put on a men's weekend, I reluctantly attended. I showed up skeptical, defensive, and ready to test the waters. I liked Pete, but this whole thing was laden with opportunities for disaster. On the last evening of this event, I sat in the back and watched Pete and his "brothers" talk about community. I could feel my body tense. My *move against* was revving up. I finally let my foot off the brake and raised my hand. After I was called on, my words were intense and pointed, "This whole community-brotherhood thing you guys are talking about better be real. If not, everything you are talking about this weekend is bullshit." When I was done, I realized that, rather than thinking those words, I spoke them. To Pete's credit, he didn't counterpunch. Rather, as a beautiful *move toward*, he said, "Why don't you try us out, Mark, and see what you find." It couldn't be that easy, could it?

Every Wednesday for months, I brought two beers and a cigar to what Pete called "The Fire." I traveled thirty-five minutes to his backyard and watched, listened, and tested the community-brotherhood. The men were honest, vulnerable, and real. This couldn't be true. Sure, there were disagreements and challenges. Rather than fighting (my *move against* go to), they sought to talk things out. Even when there were disagreements, the man was never "out." A behavior would never move you out of the community. Contrary to what I had experienced, love doesn't do that. Love endures, love protects, love trusts. Mmm...that sounds eerily familiar to a verse in the Bible (1 Corinthians 13). Could it be true?

Patrick Davidson was one of the "brothers" in Pete's group. He was eighteen years younger than me. Gifted, smart, and strategic, with one of the best mathematical minds I have ever known. His confidence was intriguing to me. He didn't seem to have the edge that I had when I was his age. There was something genuine about him. The truth was that I wanted to label Patrick with the things that I didn't like about myself when I was his age, but I wouldn't fully recognize this until I tearfully shared with Patrick much later. Instead of choosing to *move against* Patrick, I chose to move closer to him. I wanted to hear his story and find out what made this guy tick.

As a young executive, Patrick was on the fast track in senior leadership. He was also the first businessperson I met who had heard of Robert E. Quinn, whose life mission is to inspire positive change. Quinn is a best-selling author, the cofounder of the Center for Positive Organizations at University of Michigan and a thought partner on leadership and change . Patrick had read one of Quinn's books. I had not only read a few of his books; I had also studied them, poured over the concepts, and implemented his principles of Actual Change Theory into my personal thinking and into my workshops on Transformational Leadership. They are the seedbed of everything I teach today. Because they work for me, I am a passionate evangelist.

When Patrick became a general manager of an orthopedic manufacturing company, his commitment was to build a smart and healthy organization. Early on, he invited me to partner with him as a trusted advisor to build and maintain a leadership team. We committed to the process of learning to practice the principles in the book *The Five Dysfunctions of a Team.* For years, we achieved world-class results at multiple facilities by executing the right plan with the right people in the right culture. While Patrick and I will share a love for organizational transformation for the rest of our lives, our commitment to our personal transformation is the priority. We laugh together; we cry together; we celebrate together; and, most often, we celebrate together with either Jameson or the best Bourbon we can find and a good cigar. Maybe, just maybe, this whole "community-brotherhood" thing is being redeemed! In fact, authenticity could lead to something deeper and richer.

Think about these wise words from Meister Eckhart, German theologian, philosopher, and mystic, "If the only prayer you ever say in your entire life is thank you, it will be enough." While I won't prescribe that you pray this prayer, I will suggest ways to put the intent of this prayer into practice.

Who are the people in your life that have loved you, have supported you, have encouraged you, and have been with you through thick and thin? They are more than valuable assets; they are gifts who are blessing your life. My encouragement is for you to take some extended time and write about them. My guess is that you will write about more than one thing they have done. Your writing will start with who they are, and as you spend time reflecting on them, not only will you be able to list their character traits; you will also be able to detail many interchanges and acts of kindness of which you were the recipient. If you are fortunate, you will also find ways in which they have been vulnerable with you and asked for your help. You will notice that the relationship is reciprocal, and you will notice the flow of goodness which you didn't have to orchestrate. Rather, you could just lean into the gift as you would lean into the flow on a lazy river in an innertube; just soaking in all that is good about it.

Once you finish the journal, my next encouragement is to write them a thank-you note—yes, a hand-written note. Beyond that, you may also want to schedule a time with them when can look them in the eye, vulnerably express your gratitude, and, again, soak in the joy of doing life with them.

A Grateful Life

Being grateful for other people is just one expression of a grateful heart. There is more. You can practice being grateful for all the good things that happen in your life. It's a matter of training your mind to notice the good that is around you every day. I shudder to think of how often I just "blew" through large amounts of any given day or week without truly noticing the good. Think about the good that comes to you: a meaningful conversation, a smile, a heart-felt handshake, the generosity of a gift, a person's inquiry of how you are doing, words of comfort or encouragement, and more. More than that, the gift of waking up, health, and all the "stuff" you take for granted. Don't bother keeping a list. Just notice and be grateful.

Grateful for All of Life

Once you get in the rhythm of being grateful, it becomes more of a habit. However, if you want to test the mettle of your gratefulness muscle, start being grateful for *all* that life brings you: the good and the bad, the joys and the sorrows, the successes and the failures, the

IF YOU WANT TO TEST THE METTLE OF YOUR GRATEFULNESS MUSCLE, START BEING GRATEFUL FOR *ALL* THAT LIFE BRINGS YOU affirmations and the rejections. This is certainly counterintuitive and countercultural. You would be hard-pressed to find authors writing about the importance of being grateful for any of the pains in life. However, you often hear of people who have experienced hardship express that once they come out on the other side, they wouldn't change it for anything. What in the world do they mean? They can't expect us to believe that they are better off, or can they?

I am not proposing we gleefully welcome pain or bad things in our life. It's just that they are a part of life. Susan David (*Emotional Agility*) is very clear, "Discomfort is the price of admission to a meaningful life." What if you chose to accept this premise?

Sometimes the suffering we experience is self-inflicted by our bad choices—I know that too well. Other times, bad things happen because we live in a broken world with broken people. What I am learning is that when pain (such as discomfort, challenges, and sorrows) comes our way—and it will—we have a choice of how we handle it.

One of my spiritual guides for decades, Henri Nouwen, boldly challenges, "We are only truly grateful people when we can say thank you to all that has brought us to the present moment." Yikes! I have a choice in the matter. Just as I can notice the good things and choose to be grateful, I can notice the discomforts, and, instead of avoiding them, running away from them, or numbing them, I can accept that they have happened to me—can probably be angry about them for a time—can learn to be sad about them, mourn them, and, then, eventually (and this may take a while), I can choose to be grateful for them.

There are only two options to discomfort. One reaction

is bitterness. The other response is gratitude. This isn't trite, but very real. They are two radically different choices. We only have control over how we deal with our pain.

In fact, I've been challenged to "integrate" the pain. When I first heard that, I had no idea what it meant. First, I had to look up the word: "to combine (one thing) with another so that they become a whole." What? You mean I have to combine pain into my life, and when I do, the result would be wholeness? That's absurd! That is, until I realized how often I did not integrate the pain. I did everything but integrate the pain—to be sure, I avoided the pain; I powered through the pain; I numbed the pain; and more. None of my reactions to the pain were helpful, and I was far from whole. It was a game changer for me to learn that the best option to pain was not to divide myself from it but to integrate it into my life. This integration is the way to living life with dignity.

So, if you dare, think about taking the journey to the deeper cuts of gratitude.

> THERE ONLY TWO OPTIONS TO DISCOMFORT. ONE REACTION IS BITTERNESS. THE OTHER RESPONSE IS GRATITUDE.

Breathe and Pause

List the people who have been a blessing to you, and specifically express your gratitude.

Notice the good that happens in your life every day—from the sublime to the wonderful. And when you notice, be grateful.

Explore the notion of the choice you have when experiencing bad things or pain. Consider integrating it into your life.

We cannot become who we are meant to be by remaining who we are. –MAX DE PERE

It is better to lead from behind and to put others in front, especially when you celebrate victory when nice things occur. You take the front line when there is danger. Then people will appreciate your leadership. –NELSON MANDELA

CHAPTER 12

Morphing Dynamics

One of the premiere processes for Nexecute, LLC is an intensive six-months process for training leaders. It involves a day of training each month, meeting with a mentor, homework, and the completion of a real-time project. These are conducted for people who apply and who are vetted for the training; the prerequisite is that they be "A-Players." The investment is substantial, and we find that the best ROI is for those who are high performers in the organization.

Have you ever thought about the power of "intention?" In a recent workshop, as we were taking a deeper dive into Transformational Leadership, I posed this question, "How have your intentions produced the experiences you are having now?" It is our understanding that you behave as you believe.

What flows out of your beliefs are your intentions. Therefore, your intentions produce your experiences. Most people do not behave this way. In fact, every human being is wired with the negative bias that things happen to us and that we can

HOW HAVE YOUR INTENTIONS PRODUCED THE EXPERIENCES YOU ARE HAVING NOW?

only react to what good or bad is happening around us. What if there were a different way to look at it? What if my intentions were to have such clarity on WHO I wanted to be in any given situation that I could respond according to my intentions, rather than react?

I asked them to help with this exercise. "Let's suppose that my intent, as the leader of this workshop, was to create a safe space and right processes to help people maximize their potential (This is actually my personal mission statement.) What intentions would I need to create a safe space?" Their answers were descriptive actions: attentively listen, kindly confront, ask questions, and more. I pushed them a bit further and asked them to describe the type of person who could show up with these behaviors: a person who was okay with who he or she was, a transformational person, an authentic person, and more. I asked to take it a step further, "How do you become this type of transformational person?" They quickly responded, "Self-awareness and self-management." Yes! They caught the first step of transformational journey.

I could engage and show up in the world by being rigid or transactional and by spending time reacting to situations, thereby leaking energy that is chaotic, uninspiring, unimaginative, and discouraging. Do you know anybody like that? Sure, we all are tempted to do that and to succumb to it.

On the other hand, at any given point of the day or in the seasons of my life, I can make completely different choices: to be transformative, to be clear about my intent, and to be committed to living from the inside out, thereby leaking the energy of purpose, passion, clarity, and authenticity. The more we make the latter choice, the easier it will become for us to spend more time in the transformative mind-set.

Remember Mr. Nye, the apple farmer? I fondly remember many lessons from my chores on the farm. Here is one I repeatedly share as I teach Transformational Leadership.

"How do you know if an apple tastes bad?" Don't think too hard. You must taste it. Every fall, many families go apple picking. There is nothing like loading up the kids on a sunny fall afternoon in Michigan. It's just cool enough to need a hoodie, and families drive to the apple orchard for an experience that is not found in their subdivisions. Little kids hop like bunnies, as they make the way to the hay wagon. Preteens pretend as if they are bored; however, they go along because they know that, at some level, apple picking is a family tradition they don't want to miss. The tractor driver shouts out the different areas of the orchard that might contain the type of apples you like to pick. I couldn't wait for the golden delicious section.

With bags in hand, the whole families look for the trees which will yield the scrumptious bounty. Here's the deal. When you look at the tree, you don't know if the apple tastes good. When you look at an individual apple, you don't if the apple tastes good. When you touch the apple, you still don't know if it tastes good. Of course, it could be soft or have a wormhole, so you discard it quickly. You truly don't know until you sink your teeth into nature's goodness.

In my stint on the apple farm, here's what I know: long

before my golden is delicious, it hangs on the tree for the summer, soaking in nutrients from the tree itself and from nature. In the spring of the year, it shows up as a bud. If you ever want a spectacular sight, visit orchards in the spring. My hometown still celebrates the Blossomtime Festival. During the winter, the branch which holds the apple receives nutrients from the trunk of the tree, which gathers life from the root system. This is the purpose of pruning. I've been part of the pruning of branches, as well as part of the tearing out of the entire root system. You've heard of the term "bad apple"? A bad apple comes from a bad tree; when something is wrong, every part of the tree is suspect.

> IF WE ARE NOT CAREFUL, WE WILL TASTE LIKE BAD APPLES. I AM NOT PROPOSING THAT WE THROW PEOPLE AWAY. THE POINT OF THE ANALOGY IS THAT WHEN PEOPLE GET AROUND US, THEY WILL EXPERIENCE WHAT IS INSIDE OF US. IT WILL EITHER TASTE GOOD OR TASTE BAD.

If we are not careful, we will taste like bad apples. I am not proposing that we throw people away. The point of the analogy is that when people get around us, they will experience what is inside of us. It will either taste good or taste bad.

Bad apples have something awry in their beliefs systems. Again, these are often way below the surface. In our root system, if we believe that life is about our comfort, then we will react to anything and anybody who tries to take away our comfort. Think of the way we react when someone cuts us off while we are driving. If the trunk of our tree isn't solid, we make decisions based on what other people think. It's all to seek some level of validation that I am enough or that I am okay. What we purchase, what we drive, what we wear, or how we lead is influenced by what others think. These two beliefs will yield fruit that truly doesn't taste good; life becomes "all about me." It has characteristics of narcissism: selfishness, lack of compassion, little empathy, being right, being divisive, bullying, and more. The essence of this tree is that "I am just fine the way I am. Leave me alone." It is about control and being rigid. It is transactional.

A good apple has a different belief system. In the root system, if we believe that life is about having purpose, then no matter what comes our way, we are clear about WHO we are and WHY we are here. Life will not be easy, and there will be detours, but they will not change us at our core. If the trunk of our tree is solid, then we will have clarity about our values and make principled decisions. When we are off base, we will course-correct because we have clear boundaries. The environment doesn't matter, because our purpose and our passion drive us. These two beliefs will yield good fruit; life now becomes a way of serving others. It has the characteristics of compassion, kindness, empathy, collaboration, win-win, and more. The essence of this tree is that "I am open" to whatever I need to do to become even more transformative. Are you open to making big changes in your life?

THE ENVIRONMENT DOESN'T MATTER, BECAUSE OUR PURPOSE AND OUR PASSION DRIVE US.

This isn't about perfection; it is about having a clarity about the ways you want to show up in the world. Martin Luther

King, Jr., Jesus Christ, Mahatma Gandhi, Mother Teresa, and Nelson Mandela modeled this for us. We live in a time when we can study these men and women and how they became transformative leaders. *Harvard Business Review* just featured an article entitled, "Lincoln and the Art of Transformative Leadership." Author Doris Kearns Goodwin writes of the challenges Lincoln endured that built his character and wisdom to guide the Emancipation Proclamation. "Possessed of a powerful emotional intelligence, Lincoln was both merciful and merciless, confident and humble, patient and persistent."

You don't have to be featured in the history books to be a Transformational Leader. It can happen every day in homes, clubs, schools, work groups, factories, and board rooms. You notice I wrote, "It 'can' happen." It can, but it often does not happen. Maybe the reason the list of people above is highlighted is that they were so different from other key influencers. They didn't follow the crowd. They were change agents who lived transformative lives, all with a furious passion.

Breathe and Pause

How do you live your life?

Are you clear about your purpose?

Do you know your core values?

Can you identify your unique strengths and how they are instrumental in living out of your personal mission?

Conflict can and should be handled constructively; when it is, relationships benefit. –Harriet B. Braiker

Remember that what gets talked about and how it gets talked about determines what will happen. Or won't happen. And that we succeed or fail, gradually then suddenly, one conversation at a time. –Susan Scott

CHAPTER 13

The "No Conflict" Rule

"We need conflict resolution skills," is an oft-repeated phrase I get from executives. The more I probe, the more I realize that while most leaders believe conflict is important, they avoid it at almost every level. Most behave as if conflict can and should be circumvented. Therefore, few leaders or, for that matter, few human beings handle conflict well, professionally or personally. I have watched gifted and successful leaders mishandle conflict by avoiding the topic, not being straight forward, being ambiguous or shifty, by screaming, stewing, or by telling white lies or half-truths. All these actions are barriers to building healthy relationships and achieving successful long-term results.

Let's be clear: conflict is natural and inevitable in any

relationship, especially in a work environment. In fact, healthy debate—disagreement, challenge, conflict—is good for learning, innovation, productivity, and deepening relationships. What I had to learn was constructive, healthy conflict.

For too much of my life, I lived with two diametrically opposed themes: "no conflict" versus "mastering conflict." They describe the continuum of My Conflict Profile. I would never have guessed that now I teach people how to master conflict, even going so far as to have individuals and teams write out their individual and team Conflict Profile. The narrative of our life has a meta-narrative; one is our Conflict Profile. This is a long way from how I learned how to handle conflict.

I grew up in a home where it was ultimately stated, "There will be no more conflict." Because I was a *move against*, you can almost imagine my reaction to that declaration. An insecure *move against* for years picked the fights at home, made jabs to get a reaction, and eventually learned that doing so was the only way for some semblance of the truth to see the light of day. I carried that way of relating into adulthood. If people weren't going to tell me the truth, I could sense the bullshit and wanted to expose it. I often did this will little kindness and great sarcasm; I didn't see how my truth grenades exposed pierced hearts with their shrapnel even as they laid bare the truth I had been seeking.

While it may surprise people who know me, I didn't like conflict. I would much rather get along with you. It's just that my style of relating, fueled by my low-self-esteem, had driven varying levels of conflict wherever I went. In fact, a man who knew me for years once blurted, "Why does conflict seem to follow you wherever you go?" I was both surprised and sad. I didn't want that reputation…and, when my BS meter went off, what was I supposed to do? Stay silent? Nope!

When my dad finally laid down the "no conflict" ultimatum, I was disappointed, but I could hear it as an adult male and could respond with a kind, yet firm, truth. Just to set the stage: my children were teenagers, and I was an adult (age forty-eight), when my dad called my sister and me into a private meeting for the declaration.

Imagine that, after every one of these statements, my dad simply said, "No conflict!"

"Dad, you really don't want that; conflict is emotionally healthy."

"Having no conflict is not good for relationships."

"Conflict allows us to understand each other and to solve problems."

"Conflict helps us learn how to be angry in a healthy way."

"Conflict makes our family stronger."

"If you choose 'no conflict,' you will never have a deep, authentic relationship with me, my wife, or your grandchildren."

The son who fought his parents his whole life had decided that fighting was over. I love my parents. I have honored their wishes. And every one of my sentences in my response to my dad's "no conflict" rule has come to pass in my extended family.

My immediate family is quite different. We are learning how to lean into conflict and, in fact, to master it. We don't relish in it; we just know that we need to lean into the discomfort of it. We don't run from it; we stand in it to honor each other. We are so much better off, so much healthier because we do.

My son graduated with a communications major at Central

Michigan University, and, in one of his classes, he studied the role of conflict. He couldn't imagine the "no conflict" rule, because he had learned in practice, and now in principle. that conflict is, first, a given in all relationships; that, second, conflict is healthy for relationships; and that, third, it must be entered courageously. There is both an art and a science of handling conflict.

Mining for Truth

What is ironic is that, in my role as a trusted advisor for organizations, I mine for conflict, because that is where the gold is. It is intrinsic to leadership. Truth is often buried in caves of mistrust, pain, disillusionment, and negativity. Sometimes, to get to the truth, I use a pickax, and, other times, I use dynamite. My belief is that the truth will set us free. My intent is that the most compassionate thing I can do for you is to get to the truth in a kind way. Even once the truth is mined, it needs to be tested in the fire so that the dross can be removed to get to the highest grade of gold. Both processes can be uncomfortable—okay, even painful. The end results are so worth it.

> EVEN ONCE THE TRUTH IS MINED, IT NEEDS TO BE TESTED IN THE FIRE SO THAT THE DROSS CAN BE REMOVED TO GET TO THE HIGHEST GRADE OF GOLD.

The #1 Rule of Conflict: "Do Not Vent!"

Can't I just vent and move on?

I'll often get the question about venting. It seems that venting has developed as a somewhat acceptable way to avoid having hard conversations. People say, "Let me just vent and get it 'off my chest.'" I would propose that, rather than helping conflict, venting is detrimental to conflict resolution. It fuels the fire of whatever is burning. Rather than dousing out the fire with the water of resolution, venting provides more heat for the fire to expand, by giving space to discharge the pain and the anger that people feel. Most of the time, the venting is gossiping that is really blaming. Here is what the researchers know to be true: "Blame kills relationships and organizational cultures. It's toxic. It's also a go-to reaction for many of us." (Brené Brown—*Rising Strong*) Rather than suffocating the fire, venting also provides the oxygen to expand the fire, by creating sides of an issue and by solidifying the impression that, by venting, the problem is now solved. Such is not the case.

If you have a problem with someone, go to them personally and confront them. Doing it literally means to stand in front with someone; to survey what each of them see as the reality and to talk it out. Commit to connecting instead of avoiding. Seek to understand. Conflict resolution is both a science and a skill to develop.

Four Conflict Mind-Sets

1. People want to know the truth. While the truth may hurt—yes, people skirt around as if they are walking on thin ice—people just want the honest truth. Give them the dignity of that gift.

2. People want to be heard. Learning to master any form of conflict is not a monologue. It's a dialogue between people who have made a commitment to truly listen to one another.

3. Truth is based on perception. Just because I see the situation one way doesn't mean I have the whole story. In fact, I have only my perception of the situation. Remember, there are different vantage points in any relationship.

4. All people need to own their "t"— truths. Once I understand that I can only share my perception, I need to remember that my perception is not a universal "law"— not the capital "T" truth. The key is to offer my truth and to create space for other people to offer their truths. If you agree, great. If not, each small "t" truth needs to be explored further.

Seeking to Understand

As I continue to develop the art of conflict, I adopt methods, depending on the circumstance and the person. I have learned to ask for permission. My friends mock me when I ask, "Can I push into that?" or, "Are you open?" "Do you want dig a little deeper?" or, "Is that the last 10 percent, or is there something more?" Most often, people let me. They jokingly regret it and ultimately are grateful. Some have gone so far as to thank me for fighting for the truth. How's that for a different energy for a *move against*? From fighter for myself to fighter for the truth, with the intention of caring for others.

Deb and I reflect on the question asked of me over twenty-five years ago, "Why does conflict seem to follow you wherever you go?" My actions were not always helpful or kind. However, my intentions were clear. Not facing the truth

Not facing the truth is destructive to relationships.

is destructive to relationships. It doesn't feel like freedom, because it isn't freedom. The reason conflict "followed me" is that my meter for untruth—posing, faking, inauthenticity, even lying about how a person feels—spikes to the red zone. With the time I have left on this Earth, I don't want to or need to spend my time being duplicitous. I tried that and proved a hundred times over that it doesn't work. I would much rather be around people of truth or helping people live in the truth. That is where freedom lives: both in mourning over struggles and in celebrating things that are good.

How do I show up for organizations and for my coaching clients? As someone who speaks the kind truth. As someone who wants to help people transform and, maybe, just maybe, learn how to embrace and to master conflict. How do you show up when there is conflict?

Breath and Pause

What is your Conflict Profile?

How are you practicing the Four Conflict Mind-Sets?

All of business and all of life is about relationships.
Phenomenal leaders understand that humans are starving for
*authentic relationships. –*HOWARD PARTRIDGE

The greatness of a community is most accurately
measured by the compassionate actions of its members.
*–*CORETTA SCOTT KING

CHAPTER 14

Community Is Messy

For all the wonderful benefits of being in community with people, it is just plain messy. Reread that sentence, and sit with it for a minute.

There are layers of both the benefit and the bane of community. As I write, I am aware that stirring deeply within me is a "love-hate" relationship with a community. That's vulnerable. Of course, I believe in the importance of community. And I know that once I choose to live in community, it will stretch me and aggravate me at every level of my being.

If you believe Dr. Brene Brown in her initial TEDx Houston Talk and subsequent writings, we really can't and shouldn't avoid community, "Community is why we are all here." The challenge is how we show up to community; maintaining our autonomy, while being interdependent. These are not mutually exclusive. Rather, they are guidelines for living in authentic community: "It...requires us to be vulnerable, get uncomfortable, and learn how to be present with people without sacrificing who we are" (*Braving the Wilderness*).

What do I mean by autonomous interdependence?

- I am gifted with a set of strengths and choose to humbly and confidently serve, while contributing to the success of something greater than myself.

- I am an integral part of the whole, where I serve with my strengths and manage my weaknesses, while, at the same time, joining with others who serve with their strengths, thereby jointly contributing to the sustainable success of something great.

We will have different circles of community in our life. No matter the depth of authenticity, there seem to be principles that apply.

Let me clarify the opposites of interdependence, which are not the marks of a healthy community:

- Codependence: I need you to meet a deeper need—I serve you so that you serve me!

- Dependence: I need you to recognize and support me—you serve me!

To enter community in a healthy way, we must be

> TO ENTER COMMUNITY IN A HEALTHY WAY, WE MUST BE INTENTIONAL ABOUT BEING AUTONOMOUS: KNOWING WHO WE ARE PRECEDES WHAT WE DO.

intentional about being autonomous: knowing WHO we are precedes WHAT we do. Otherwise, we will look to our community members to validate us and to try to get from them what they cannot and should not give us.

When I think about it, I still have, a residual "love-hate" relationship with community. I know how important it is. I espouse the benefits of it. I accept the research around it. So what's my problem? I don't like it that community is so hard. It takes so much effort. Here's what I know to be true.

Five "I" Statements of Community

1. I need community. Because I am made for community and thrive best while in community, I need it. I am a better person when I am part of an authentic community.

2. I want to be in control. Community requires me to loosen the grip of control. And I don't know about you, but I like being in control. To state it as a double negative: I don't like not being control. It's not that I give up all control. Rather, it's that I must admit that I do not control others and that I behave in a way that I do not control others.

3. I am required to be vulnerable. Yikes! Vulnerability is not comfortable. It comes from the Latin word meaning "to wound"—if I am vulnerable you now have the information to wound me. Community will only be as rich and rewarding to the extent of how vulnerable I am willing to be.

4. I must maintain my autonomy. While I am required to be vulnerable, community doesn't mean that I lose myself, share intimate details with others, or give people

full access to every area of my life.

5. I must set healthy boundaries. Boundaries are lines of demarcation. They allow a person to determine what is allowed and not allowed in "this space."

I grew up without clear boundaries. Not only did I let others determine my worth; I also gave them too much access to my life. It showed up as codependency. My happiness was determined by others. It is an unhealthy and exhausting way to live. Setting boundaries allows me to be free and offer myself to others with an attitude of interdependence. To help me discern what is healthy and in turn, how to show up in my relationships, my mantra is: I want to be authentic with everyone. I want to be transparent with fewer. I want to be intimate with a few.

> I WANT TO BE AUTHENTIC WITH EVERYONE. I WANT TO BE TRANSPARENT WITH FEWER. I WANT TO INTIMATE WITH A FEW.

The Pursuit of Community

What is your ideal community? What would it be like? Who would be in your community? What guidelines would you like to follow?

We rarely think about these questions, much less answer them. In my effort to learn about community, I was introduced to Robert E. Quinn and his picture of a "productive community." This picture describes not only my personal community, but it can also describe a workplace that is built on trust. Healthy work environments can be communities. In these types of communities, people tend to be more inner-directed and other-focused, adopting more of a servant mentality. Quinn pushes the envelope even further: "People in productive communities also have another unusual characteristic. They want to be connected to reality. They want to know what is real, even if the news is bad." (*Change the World*) If people really want to know the truth, then truth must be spoken, accepted, and practiced. This will undoubtedly make community messy.

Community is not always comfortable, and, certainly, it is not easy. We are only human, and we bring all of those aspects with us to being part of it. In community, there will be acceptance and betrayal. Community will propel us to heights of celebration and drive us to the depths of anger and disappointment. Henri Nouwen declares, "As soon as you have community, you have a problem." The closer you get to people, the more you begin to see and experience their flaws and foibles. Worse yet, what you despise in yourself you will see in others, and it will trigger anger. And what others despise in themselves will trigger them. Yes, there are times when you will be the betrayer, the one who disappointments.

> COMMUNITY IS NOT ALWAYS COMFORTABLE, AND, CERTAINLY, IT IS NOT EASY.

I think one of the healthiest things a community can do is to have regular discussions about how to engage in healthy community. This should happen, especially in the early formation of any community.

Can you imagine if the conversation started something like the following?:

I am so glad you are becoming part of this community. You are not only aligning with us; you are also becoming a part of us. You bring special gifts, insights, and perspectives that will broaden us, and we will do the same for you. And…there will be times we will fail you.

Let's be clear: it is not "if" we fail you, but "when" we fail you. Therefore, it's important you know what this means and how to move through it. When we hurt each other, and we do, it's important for the one who is hurt to be courageous enough to go the person and to state what has happened to the offender, not gossiping to everyone else but going directly to the one who has betrayed you. It is not easy. It never is. Yet it is the only way community really works. As part of that discussion, our hope is that those who have disappointed you will own their shit. If they don't, then it's important to invite other people along with you. Fortunately, this second step hasn't happened yet in our community.

Once people are made aware of how they hurt you, the proper response is something like, "I own that. It wasn't my intent. I apologize."

The response of those who are hurt is not, "It's okay," or, "No problem." (It was not okay, and it was a problem.) The response is, "I forgive you." Those words are important. To forgive comes from the Latin word meaning to "let go." Those who are hurt declare the truth that they are willing to release the other people from the burden, thereby releasing the other people and themselves from the impact. They are willing to state clearly that they are making the move toward healing. Forgiveness is the glue that holds community together.

Some of you may be thinking that this type of conversation

sounds stilted or manufactured. Please read the paragraphs again. What this language does is create a healthy boundary for community. Most of us have grown up in a family without boundaries, and we live in a world without boundaries. Initially, boundaries seem odd and unnecessary. However, this type of boundary for relationships is about giving a sense of safety and frees people to relax and be more fully themselves.

As someone who grew up with little-to-no boundaries, I had no idea what boundaries were and why they were important. When Dr. Henry Cloud wrote about them, I was stunned. The more I studied them, the more I realized that boundaries are essential in our personal life and our business life. As leaders, we are the lynchpins for boundaries, "As a leader, you are always going to get a combination of two things: What you create and What you allow." (*Boundaries for Leaders*) Good community that is rich, kind, caring, empathic, understanding, and more doesn't just happen. Leaders need to provide space—a container, if you will—for this type of behavior. It involves providing space for all this good to happen and making sure that when the bad tries to infiltrate the space, it is confronted.

In this type of community, we can learn to release our self-will, to transcend our EGO, and to learn to live with and for others. It is the garden where humility is nurtured.

In this type of community, we become really exposed. What is revealed are deep layers of jealousy, anger, cynicism, feelings of rejection, abandonment, and more. Being autonomous in a community means that I cannot put unfair expectations on people that they will not trigger these deep layers within me. Moreover, I cannot expect people in a community to validate me—giving me my sense of worth. I cannot expect that it will always be fun or peaceful.

Community is not about harmony. It is about space where we can try to love and be loved, serve and be served, know and be known, celebrate and be celebrated. It's about engaging in one another's lives and truly getting to know one another. It's based on vulnerability. It's about having the right intention, connecting the dots to live in congruence with ourselves and authentically with others, sincerely engaging so that all people feel as if they are in this together.

> COMMUNITY IS NOT ABOUT HARMONY. IT IS ABOUT SPACE WHERE WE CAN TRY TO LOVE AND BE LOVED, SERVE AND BE SERVED, KNOW AND BE KNOWN, CELEBRATE AND BE CELEBRATED.

One of the men in my close community puts it this way. When someone in the community shares a burden and is hurting, the rest of the community feels the pain and empathizes. We don't take the burden: we help carry the burden. In doing so the pain is distributed to the community at some level, and the burden is a bit lighter. When some people in the community share their joys, the rest of the community is lifted to the height of those people's joys; there is affirmation, confirmation, rejoicing, and reflections of goodness. The joy is exponentially amplified! It makes no sense mathematically. It makes complete sense relationally.

Only Transformational People Can Be in Real Community

For decades, I wondered why this type of community was so elusive for me. Now I know why; I couldn't show up authentically. It would have been detrimental to me, and I would have wounded so many others in what little community I formed along the way. Transactional people don't understand and don't do well in healthy community. Transformative people can. The wonder and miracle of community is that the community multiplies the transformation. What a gift!

By nature, community connects individuals. It's denoted in the root and suffix of the word—"common-unity"—there is something in common. This bond is why community exists and the reason for the thread that holds it together. Its purpose can be about dreams for the future or about wanting to change a current modality that is harmful.

A word of caution, though, when the message of any community is focused on a premise of some form of antagonism: what community members are against. At first, this sounds appealing. It is, after all, whatever binds them together. However, without clear boundaries and a core value that all people matter and deserve dignity, the community can easily cultivate a mind-set of exclusivity that leads to certainty. This is toxic. Rhetoric and behavior become transactional, in that it creates a win-lose proposition. Messages of unity are built around "us" being right and "them" being wrong. Please take this at face value. I am all for the importance of being aware of what draws people together and makes them connected to a tribe. The danger lies not in the commonality; rather, it lies in the finger-pointing, hatred-filled judgmentalism that dismisses the humanity of those outside of the "common union" and that vilifies them. Way too much of the religious and political culture engages this way, and it is divisive, dismissive, mean, and dehumanizing.

The healthy intention of any community is best served

when it is formed on and stays focused on the premise of what moves the community to the collective good, away from EGO and cultivating a deeper sense of service and dignity.

No wonder Brian Grazer wrote, "Curiosity is the key to authentic connection" (A Curious Mind).

One such community for me is True Pursuit, a men's ministry with the focus on rescuing men's hearts and offering them freedom. My community are men who meet every other week to check in with the vulnerable question, "How's your heart?" We believe that our best gift to each other is our own spiritual and emotional health that is fostered in solitude. That way, when we come together, our community reflects our solitude. Out of our community flows a joint mission. We are clear about our purpose and committed to living out the stated core values. I love them. I trust them. I am grateful for each of them.

As you may guess, even this community is messy. It is maintained by living out the five "I" statements listed earlier in this chapter. I changed the pronoun to emphasize that each of us must believe these to be true.

Five "We" Statements of Community

1. We need community. We have been in community for many years and regularly ask the question, "What drives us to community?" Our conclusion is desperation and perseverance. We long for it at such deep levels that it could be called desperation. We want it so badly that we will arrange schedules and navigate detours, persevering through whatever obstacles get in the way of community.

2. We want to be in control, so we practice self-control. We

are aware of how community stretches us. We can't be in real community and not have rubs, disappointments, or even betrayal. At these junctures, we make the choice to forgive—sometimes more quickly than others. Yet that is the choice that we must, and that we do make.

3. We are required to be vulnerable. Faking isn't allowed. Actually, it's not tolerated. We "go after" each other with a tenacious love, because we trust each other's hearts. We find that it's just easier to be vulnerable than to pose.

4. We maintain autonomy. We know when we can show up authentically—hurting or healthy. We also believe that we are responsible for our spiritual and emotional life and that, therefore, we do not look at each other for validation. Rather, in community, we receive affirmation, encouragement, comfort, challenge, and celebration.

5. We set healthy boundaries. We give each other access to our lives and work hard to clarify healthy boundaries so that we maintain our autonomy and live interdependently.

Breathe and Pause

What would it mean if you were part of a community like the one described?

What does "being autonomous" mean to you?

What would it take for you to be part of an interdependent community?

How do you relate to the five "I" statements of community? What would it mean if you adopted the five "we" statements?

It is through gratitude for the present moment that the spiritual dimension of life opens up. –ECKHART TOLLE

Learning to live in the present moment brings about a shift in our perception, rather than a mere change in our behavior. –SHANNON DUNCAN

CHAPTER 15

Present-Moment Living

What if it were true that the best moment you experience is the moment you are in right now? Present-moment living is the awareness and appreciation for the life we have right now; it may be easy, difficult, pleasant, or it may be challenging. No matter how you describe it, the gift is this moment.

After all, this the only moment you have. The past is never coming back. The future is out there. Therefore, to live in the past or the future is to literally lose your life.

This was a difficult principle for me to grasp. Given my story, I was always wishing the past was better, and, at the same time, I was always looking for the next moment to be even better yet: a better person to talk to, a better conversation, a better thrill, and more.

Yesterday is past. That makes it over, irretrievably gone. Yet so many people live there. Are you living in the past? Maybe you are, but only sometimes. For some, the glory they once had in the past is how they want to be remembered in the present moment. You know them; every story is about their glory days or about their accomplishments. I am in favor of reminiscing and celebrating the past. I am not in favor of living in the past. For others, the stories of their past are filled with sorrow, anger, or resentment. They are ridden with envy over those who had it better, and many sentences begin with, "If only..." as they wish how things were different. Sure, we can learn from our past, but to live there is maddening. I know too many people who spend most of their present moments in wasted energy, unnecessary stress, and self-imposed suffering, because they can't let go of the past. It reminds me of U2's "Stuck in a Moment You Can't Get Out Of":

You've got to get yourself together

You've got stuck in a moment

And now you can't get out of it

Don't say that later will be better

Now you're stuck in a moment

And you can't get out of it.

I spent too many years of my life in various forms of this state. It's not appealing. While I don't like to admit it, it's a victim mentality. This is such a dysfunctional mind-set because it overrides personal responsibility. I ended up living life too many times as a spectator, convinced that my one-and-only life was beyond my control. I envied those who, in my mind, "got" to play on the field of their own lives.

Rather than taking personal responsibility and showing

LITTLE DID THEY KNOW THAT THEIR ACTIONS GAVE ME MORE REINFORCEMENT TO MY VICTIMHOOD. IT'S MANIPULATION AT ITS MOST ABSURD.

up with dignity, I had a gnawing sense that I had to prove something. I was unaware of what it was. This unsettling in my spirit could be experienced by what I might describe as an "edge"—sometimes sharp, sometimes bitter, sometimes self-promoting, sometimes self-deprecating. This is the by-product of being a transactional person. It's protocol is to believe other people should notice me, feel sorry for me, or lavish me with some type of attention. Here's the transactional equation: I get the attention I need because people try to help me by telling me their sad stories or by offering pious platitudes. Little did they know that their actions gave me more reinforcement to my victimhood. It's manipulation at its most absurd.

The other dangerous word that flies in the face of the present-moment living is "tomorrow." It's living with a mind-set that tomorrow will give me something different because it owes something to me. Tomorrow, I will win the lotto. Tomorrow, work will miraculously have no problems. Tomorrow, my neighbors will move. "Tomorrow…"—you fill in the blank. You end up worrying about tomorrow or hoping that it will yield different results than today. This is different than being hopeful; it's more about being anxious, unsettled, almost unnerved, fretting so much that you miss the present moment.

How many times have you spent stuck in the past or waiting on the future? I wonder now how many times I walked away from pleasant experiences just because I couldn't wait for something better to happen to me tomorrow. More times than I would like to admit. It was an ugly sense of resolve that resulted in shrugs of the shoulder and obnoxious eye rolls.

In either extreme, I missed what was right in front of me. I did not want to accept "what is." As a move against and someone with a warped belief system, I would fight "what is," be angry with "what is," try to manipulate "what is," and more. It was all about having some perception of control. Mind you, I didn't have control. It was the perception of control. I was mentally forcing things for my benefit. Truly, transactional.

Then I read the convicting words of Shannon Duncan's *Present Moment Living:* "Letting go of how we wish things were or believe them to be in favor of becoming aware of how things really are is an imperative step toward personal freedom." I wasn't free. I had carried the chains of this slavery my whole life. I was exhausted and ready to make the change. I could spend the last half of my life futilely wanting something different or learning to live in the present moment.

Of course, step one in any form of addiction, and I was addicted, is to admit that you have a problem. "Hi! My name is Mark. I have a problem of not living in the present moment…I don't accept 'what is.'" Steps two and three were becoming a new habit for me: turning another one of my issues over to God. The next steps in my recovery sucked. The ruthless inventory was tiring. Reflecting on the impact it had on my family was excruciating. I wanted to get to steps eleven and twelve quickly (I am an achiever). However, to short-circuit the healing would have kept me at the surface of the problem and not gotten me to the real issue: my limiting beliefs. "If you don't change your beliefs, your life will be the like this forever," writes Dr. Robert Anthony.

Pivot Points to Present-Moment Living

Without boring you with too many details, I can safely say that at the core of not living in the present moment was not accepting "what is." Have you ever wished things were different? It was a space I had been trapped in. My first step was to let go of how I had wished things were different. Rather than fighting reality, it meant accepting reality. Once the belief would change, so would my behavior. Second, I could begin the process of learning how to respond to reality instead of reacting. Reacting is associated with fighting. Responding is associated with mindful choices. That's it. Now I could make the third pivot: to choose to live life mindfully. Many situations in life are out of my control. My response to the situations is fully within my control. Would I choose to exercise the muscle of my will? To do so would make my life enriching and meaningful. I would have a sense of empowerment to face any reality with curiosity. My intentions in any given moment would impact my experiences.

During this season, I was introduced to the ancient Greek word "kairos," another word for "time." Our lifespan is measured in time, or chronology, from "Kronos," the ancient Greek word which refers to sequential or linear time. In ancient Greek mythology, the god Chronos was pictured as elderly, gray-haired, and bearded, and was the personification of time. No wonder we talk about "Father Time."

In the ordinary experiences of our lives, we can either move through life mindfully, a place of peace, or mindlessly, which is the birthplace of apathy and boredom. If we choose, we can seize opportunities to see ordinary moments—reality—from a different lens. Kairos is the different lens. It is considered as the "now" time, the time of decision. Kairos is the right moment of opportunity which requires proactivity to achieve success. The ancient Greeks believed that kairos could intersect with Kronos, regular time.

In a scene from *Dead Poets Society*, Professor John Keating—played by the late Robin Williams—challenges his boarding school English students in the scene where they sheepishly stand in front of the trophy case, peering inquisitively into the photographs of alumni. The professor speaks with a deliberate tone about the boys in the faded black-and-white photographs:

> They're not that different from you, are they? Same haircuts. Full of hormones, just like you. Invincible, just like you feel. The world is their oyster. They believe they're destined for great things, just like many of you; their eyes are full of hope, just like you. Did they wait until it was too late to make from their lives even one iota of what they were capable? Because, you see gentlemen, these boys are now fertilizing daffodils. But if you listen real close, you can hear them whisper their legacy to you. Go on, lean in. Listen, you hear it?
>
> Carpe! Hear it?
>
> Carpe! Carpe diem! Seize the day, boys. Make your lives extraordinary.

I wept when I first watched that scene in 1989. I didn't know why. I do now. I didn't know how to seize the kairos moments. Now, I am free to respond to each moment. It is within my control of how I want to show up, no matter what reality is in front of me.

Apparently, I missed the point of the lyrics to the Byrds' "Turn! Turn! Turn!"

To everything (Turn! Turn! Turn!)

There is a season (Turn! Turn! Turn!)

And a time to every purpose, under Heaven.

Once my beliefs began to change, I started accepting "what is." The way I show up to the world now is completely different. I continue to learn from my wife how to live in the present moment. She is a master at it. I am learning from her that free-flowing emotions are beautiful and that sometimes no words are needed. More often, when I experience

...sorrow, I mourn.

...happiness, I smile.

...goofiness, I laugh.

...healing, I am grateful.

...goodness, I celebrate.

...compassion, I am tender.

...companionship, I embrace.

...someone else sharing, I listen.

...having to say "good-bye," I cry and let go.

...silence, I am quiet.

...love, I soak it in.

...playfulness, I delight.

I am far from perfect. I can tell you this freedom is so much better than slavery.

From scarcity to abundant mentality, from transaction to transformation, I get to choose how to show up and to participate in my life.

Breathe and Pause

What would it mean for you to embrace each present moment as a gift?

How are you tempted to live in the past?

How are you tempted to live in the future?

How are doing at accepting "what is?"

*A mentor is someone who allows you to see the hope
inside yourself.* —OPRAH WINFREY

*If I have seen further, it is by standing on the
shoulders of giants.* —ISAAC NEWTON

CHAPTER 16

The Benefit of Experience (Mentoring and Coaching)

"You should have breakfast with Marty."

In my late twenties my career was skyrocketing, and I wasn't sure why I needed to meet with a man in his mid-sixties. After all, how could he relate to me. As a young transactional leader, I wasn't sure what my "win" would be. I shake my head in disgust now, as I relate these immature mental gymnastics. Oh my, I had so much to learn.

Marty was gracious and wise in our meeting. He showed up to offer me space to share. I am sure that I talked incessantly, and I am not sure how many questions I asked this man who had so much to offer this young upstart. What I remember is this phrase, "Mark, you have many gifts. I would consider figuring out what is your area of interest—what do you want to do—and focus there. You don't want to spend your career being a jack-of-all-trades and a master of none." Talk about wise! If only, yes, if only I had asked him about what he meant or had been self-aware enough to dig deeper, I would have saved myself years of heartache. Now, I get it.

Marty was my first mentor…and a good one.

Merriam-Webster's dictionary defines a mentor as someone who teaches or gives help and advice to a less-experienced person in order to set an example for excellence.

The term "mentor" comes from ancient Greek mythology. In Homer's *Odyssey*, Mentor was a good friend of Odysseus. He was entrusted with the care of Odysseus' household, including the raising and teaching of his son, Telemachus.

Mentor was well known for his honesty, integrity, friendship, gentleness, kindness, and a willingness to speak forcefully, if need be. His goal was to help Telemachus become the man he wanted to be by giving him ideas, direction, and loving support.

ALL PEOPLE HAVE THE POTENTIAL TO BE MENTORS. IT TAKES TENACIOUS WORK TO BECOME GOOD MENTORS, THOSE WHO TRULY KNOW THEMSELVES.

Ever since the ancient myth was told, the word "mentor" has been used to describe a wise and trusted advisor or guide, someone who shares personal wisdom and the benefit of experience. Mentors are those who have walked roads before and who are willing and excited to support those who are walking similar roads in order to cheer them on, to encourage them with the life lessons they learned, and to accelerate the learning process. They can teach, be friends, advise, or help.

All people have the potential to be mentors. It takes tenacious work to become good mentors, those who truly know themselves. Self-knowledge is essential for mentors to give their best in their service to mentees.

Mentoring versus Coaching

When I train mentors, I am quick to clarify the actions of a mentor as opposed to those of a coach. This is not to be prescriptive in practice. Rather, it is to clarify the intent of the role.

The practice of a coach is reflected by the intention of coaching. A coach has the intention of helping the coachee produce results, whether personally or professionally. The work of the coach is more proactive, discovering where the coachee wants to go. It's also about process, identifying the steps needed to achieve the goal. This involves planning, checking, adjusting, and planning again.

Think of athletic coaches. They are very clear on the fundamentals for success. They make sure that, every step along the way, the fundamentals are honed and perfected. More than that, the coaches carefully watch their athletes. At the appropriate time, coaches instruct, train, evaluate, admonish, challenge, and inspire their athletes to further actions…all of this is done in the spirit of flawless execution.

Business coaching doesn't have a long history. In 2009, Eric Schmidt, then CEO of Google, announced that the best advice he got from an executive was to get a coach. Like so many, Schmidt wondered why he needed a coach and if he was doing something wrong. At that same time, I was getting ready to start my coaching practice and often referenced this story. Then I read *Never Eat Alone* by Keith Ferrazzi: "Successful people know they can't be their best unless they have a good coach in their corner." The tide was turning, and having a coach was no longer a stigma; rather, it was a competitive advantage for excellence, both personally and professionally.

To sum it up, in contrast, mentors are available. They have a deep well of knowledge and experience to provide, but the mentee owns the agenda and asks the questions. Mentors are a resource for the growth and change; but the onus of the process is not on them. A coach ensures that the coachee reaches the desired goal, owning the process and ensuring implementation; they are active. A mentor gives time, shares experience as asked, but they watch the process unfold as driven by their mentee.

As a coach, I get to live out my personal mission: to create safe spaces and right processes for people to maximize their potential, as I invite them to transformational living. Notice the two intentions: safe spaces and right processes.

> It's my intent is to ensure that my relationship with my clients is built on trust; therefore, the relationship is psychologically and emotionally safe. It's about being attuned and compassionate.

> It's my intent is to move my clients forward with processes that work. It's not about meeting my agenda; rather, it's about using what I have learned to help them meet their agendas. It's about being relevant and truthful, knowing when to push and when to pull.

I am clearer than ever that having mentors and coaches is an important asset. Professional golfers have a cadre of coaches in multiple disciplines. They also speak of mentors, other successful golfers who are a bit more experienced and whose advice they readily seek.

Get a Mentor...Be a Mentor

Who is mentoring you, and whom are you mentoring?

WHO IS MENTORING YOU, AND WHOM ARE YOU MENTORING?

My encouragement to any leader is to seek out mentors. They don't have to been in the same business or have the same type of role. Rather, find people you respect—people of character, excellence, and discipline who can offer you advice that only comes through experience.

As I mentioned, I think the mentee should own the agenda: should come with questions to ask or situations for which you need insight. Honor the mentor's time and set up regular meetings, whether formal or informal.

I also encourage any leader to offer to be a mentor. It's astounding to me how people think that, to be mentors, they need to be quite a bit older. Mentors share from experience. You may be just a bit older or decades older. I can promise you this, right now, that there are people younger than you who would long to spend time with you. Do you believe enough in yourself to simply offer yourself to someone else and to see what happens? By the way, you will find that mentoring is a beautiful two-way street of learning, encouragement, and challenge.

One of my mentees is Trevor Ramseier. This engaging millennial entered my life a few years ago and bluntly began a conversation with, "I am not asking you to coach me. I need you to coach me." When a six-feet-five-inches young man with a powerful deep voice speaks to me with that type of passion, I listen. Of course, I'm a *move against*, so challenge accepted!

Trevor and I have spent hours together in person and over the phone, crying, laughing, celebrating, and working through crap together. I know his story, and he knows mine. Deb and I have grown to love Trevor and his wonderful wife, Amanda, and we've been a part of their transformation, individually and as a married couple. My relationship with Trevor moved from coaching to mentoring a couple of years ago. Sometimes, he has a quick question, and, other times, it's about sharing our hearts. He regularly expresses his gratitude. Here's a snippet from a recent text message: "If I haven't said thank you enough, here's another one:

> 'Some have found a mentor, they are hard to come by. Especially those who understand masculine initiation.'"

What's that worth? Priceless!

My personal and professional success would not have occurred without the role of trusted advisors, my coaches. The two words to describe my coaches are essential. They are both a person I trust, and they are willing and able to advise me.

My current coach, who happens to be both my business partner and my coach, fulfils this role in spades. Ross Slater is brilliant, clear, well-versed in people development, and has an outstanding business acumen. We trust him implicitly. The eight hours we spend with him in person every quarter are enlightening and draining. Let's be clear: conversations are not always easy. There is no soft peddling, no holding back the truth. There is empathy, but never coddling. He celebrates successes and challenges apathy and victim beliefs. Sometimes he urges, and, other times, he encourages. The goal is clear—our success; Ross makes sure we follow a process to get there.

See Appendix—*Letter to a College Student*

Breathe and Pause

Do you have a coach? Describe the experience.

Who are your mentors? What do they offer you?

Who is at least one person whom you could mentor?

If you can dream it, you can do it. –WALT DISNEY

Overcoming the odd situations with a positive mindset inculcates the virtue of strength. –ANIL KUMAR SINHA

CHAPTER 17

The Positive Choice

After decades of training the synapses in my brain to think like a victim, some new neuro pathways needed to be built—maybe redirected and probably created. As I grew to be more and more transformational, the work of Shawn Achor played a significant role in this building process. I first watched his interview with Oprah on Super Soul Sunday, after which I picked up his book *Before Happiness* and then studied his TED Talks. I soaked up as much as I could handle. Years of research on the three existing intelligences—social, emotional, and IQ—all of which have an impact on our success, revealed that there was a deeper underlying reality. "Before you feel an emotion about the world, before you connect to another person, before you begin solving a problem, you brain has already created a reality about whether success can be achieved."

I was shell-shocked. How I view reality is the key. Will I

view obstacles as dead ends or the opportunity to build new roads? It wasn't about being an optimist or a pessimist. It was far deeper than that. It was the choice to see reality with a positive mind-set. "Positive genius isn't just the amplifier of all other forms of intelligences; it's also the precursor." One doesn't ignore the obstacles or wish them away. It is the decision to do something when faced with challenges. The optimist says the glass is half-full. The pessimist says the glass is half-empty. The "positive genius" sees that there is a glass and determines if there is more water needed, they can do something about it. Then they go about doing what needs to be done. I get to be the architect of my mind-set. I get to choose the way I interpret my world. I get to create my responses to reality. So do you!

> I GET TO BE THE ARCHITECT OF MY MIND-SET. I GET TO CHOOSE THE WAY I INTERPRET MY WORLD. I GET TO CREATE MY RESPONSES TO REALITY.

This was THE major shift for me. It not only rocked my world it also solidified that this is an integral part of being transformative: in any adversity, I could choose to frame that reality and exercise the power of my will of how I want to be in that reality. I moved from "learned helplessness" to adopting a new intelligence: AQ – "Adversity Quotient." The choice is truly ours.

The term "Adversity Quotient" was coined by Paul Stoltz in his book *Adversity Quotient: Turning Obstacles into Opportunities*. It's a matter of being resilient, adopting an attitude of perseverance and learning in response to a challenging or changing environment. It includes optimism, but it's more than that. AQ is the choice to remain engaged and involved, no matter the circumstances.

For instance, legendary college basketball coach John Wooden would repeat the lesson to his players that he learned from his father: "Don't whine, don't complain, don't make excuses." Long before Achor and his team researched it, Wooden lived it.

In any given situation, it is easy to have our microscope dialed in so closely to what is in front of us that we miss the larger picture of possibilities that moment may present. I get taken out by expectations. What I know now is that healthy emotional people are keenly aware that unstated expectations are resentments waiting to happen. Rather than staying in disappointments or resentments, they make the choice to respond to the next possibility.

For instance, we plan to spend a couple of days enjoying Mackinac Island in the summer. It's four square miles of car-free tranquility. The waters of Lake Huron and Lake Michigan glisten as they meet under the sun, and it's an idyllic place to relax. Past experience here means that we stay at a bed and breakfast on the island. It means bike rides around the perimeter with frequent stops to soak up the turquoise waters. It means sipping coffee on Adirondack chairs as we watch freighters cruising through the channel. It means horse-drawn carriage rides as we listen to guides retell the island's history, evening concerts in the park, and admiring gardens that look like they're right out of a magazine. We know what to expect, and it is spectacular.

However, what do you do when it rains for two straight days?

From Learned Helpless to Developing an Adversity Quotient

My reaction years ago would have been transactional, with this internal and probably verbal outburst: "This sucks! I can't believe we are spending money, and we can't enjoy this island. Why does it always rain for us? Our friends get all the luck; it never rains for them. Blah! Blah! Blah!" I would like to say I'm exaggerating. Embarrassingly, I am not. The key words to this way of thinking for me were "always" and "never."

At this season of my life, I notice that, because of my transformation, my response is quite different: "This sucks and it is what it is! The place we're staying has a covered front porch, comfy furniture, board games, and they brew coffee all day. We've got books and our Journals; we can set up camp out on the porch and enjoy the fresh air and view. We've been tired and rushed lately, so this will give us a chance to slow down and recharge. We can relax and have a slow day here and still enjoy dinner at our favorite spot.

At any given moment, at any given time, reality can be difficult, challenging, or outright bad. The key is what choice I will make in response to the reality. I can react negatively, or I can choose to respond.

Let's get practical; that is, HOW to respond rather than react.

First, acknowledge reality. Don't sugarcoat it; don't pretend it to be different; don't wish it to be different. Stand in front of the truth.

Second, embrace reality. It doesn't mean you have to like it. The word "embrace" has a soft connotation to it. Make no mistake; accepting shitty situations is not soft. It is an act of the will to choose to surrender. For years, I hated the word "surrender." In fact, when I use the word today, people wince. It's like a four-letter word for self-made people who grow up in America. In fact, I go so far as to have people perform the physical act of rolling their hands over so that their palms face up. Rather than a clenched fist of control, it signifies the openness to surrender to the situation and be open to the possibilities.

One of my friends is also my teacher in how to surrender. He is a former Army ranger captain. After a few tours in the Middle East, he became part of the community I mentioned earlier in the book. Wow…at first, he just listened, as he tested us to see if we were trustworthy. Over the next months, he would share only bits and pieces of some of the uncertainty and horror he experienced. It was years before we broached the concept of surrender with him. The concept wasn't in his vocabulary. It wasn't in his training. We weren't sure if he even believed it as an option. There was a day when we sensed he was ready, and we risked asking him. There was a slow nod of affirmation. His first pass at surrender is now the standard joke—but it's really the reality—for most people. As Dave's fists were clenched, we offered him the opportunity to roll his hands to the palm-up position. Picture this. A six-feet-three-inches, muscle-bound, former army ranger rolling his large fists over, still clenched tight. As he begins the process of surrender, his fingers slowly loosen. It seems they are atrophied to the tight position. This is how he survived in the army. Over time, space begins to form between each finger. Then only one finger on each of shaking hands breaks free, the middle finger. He gives a hearty "bird" to surrender. After he gave a good chuckle, the rest of the fingers were released, and he rolled his hands over to the palms-up position. Dave is not alone. Most people I know, either silently, verbally, or physically, give surrender the middle finger. That is how committed we are to having control.

Third, apply your creative mind, and get curious. Figure out the next step. And by next step, I literally mean the next step. You don't have to construct a road map for your future. You simply must figure out the next step. And after that step, the next step, and so on. Before you know it, you will be full-response mode.

This path to transformation, step-by-step, will lead you to more awareness and conscious behavior. Eventually, you may just end up being grateful.

By the way, the rainy Mackinac Island experience has happened to us twice. I am so grateful for what I have learned about transformation, which translated into being grateful for rainy days. We got curious and creative, as we spent our days in one of our favorite spots on earth. The microscope was loosened, and we saw the island in new ways, from different angles—yes, from a different lens.

> AN INTEGRAL PART IN DEVELOPING NEW PATTERNS IN MAKING POSITIVE CHOICES IS TO BE AWARE WITH WHOM YOU ARE SPENDING YOUR TIME.

An integral part in developing new patterns in making positive choices is to be aware with whom you are spending your time. We often become like the five people who are closest to us. When I am around negative people—cynical, sarcastic, mean, vindictive, victim-choosing people—that energy rubs off on me. Without judging these people, I am learning to consciously spend less time with them. If it's coworkers with whom I share a space; I can do my job and be thoughtful of only spending as much time with them as needed. If it's neighbors; I can be friendly without needing to invite them to every function just because of proximity. If it's relatives; I can adjust my expectations and set up clear boundaries with limits to extended conversations. It means being very clear on the type of person I want to be and then choosing to be around those type of people who will spur me on, encourage me, challenge me in healthy ways—people who are transformational.

If you want to learn more about yourself, consider taking the VIA Inventory, formerly known as the "Values in Action Inventory." VIA focuses on your best qualities. It is regarded as a central tool of positive psychology and has been used in hundreds of research studies and taken by over 5 million people in over 190 countries. It comes with strong validation. It is created under the direction of Dr. Martin Seligman, the "father of Positive Psychology" and author of *Authentic Happiness and Flourish,* and Dr. Christopher Peterson, distinguished scientist at the University of Michigan and author of *A Primer in Positive Psychology*, and validated by Robert McGrath, Ph.D.

I found this to be affirming and insightful in helping me learn how I truly wanted to show up to my world. This was a way to help solidify my core values. To provide you an example, here are my top five results from my "Values in Action Inventory."

Top Five Values
Spirituality, sense of purpose, and faith
You have strong and coherent beliefs about the higher purpose and meaning of the universe. You know where you fit in

the larger scheme. Your beliefs shape your actions and are a source of comfort to you.

Capacity to love and be loved

You value close relations with others, in particular those in which sharing and caring are reciprocated. The people to whom you feel most close are the same people who feel most close to you.

Gratitude

You are aware of the good things that happen to you, and you never take them for granted. Your friends and family members know that you are a grateful person, because you always take the time to express your thanks.

Perspective (wisdom)

Although you may not think of yourself as wise, your friends hold this view of you. They value your perspective on matters and turn to you for advice. You have a way of looking at the world that makes sense to others and to yourself.

Social intelligence

You are aware of the motives and feelings of other people. You know what to do to fit into different social situations, and you know what to do to put others at ease.

Breathe and Pause

What would it mean for you to have a "positive choice" mind-set?

Name the five people closest to you and notice how they influence your mind-set.

What are you learning about surrender?

Beware of the barrenness of a busy life. –SOCRATES

If the devil can't get you to sin, he'll keep you busy.
–ANNE LAMOTT

CHAPTER 18

Who's Watching the Margin

By now, you know that I am a driven person. I like to accomplish tasks, complete with lists that I cross off to signify completion. In my early days as pastor and husband, I would pride myself with the amount of work I could accomplish, and I'd celebrate a calendar that was stuffed full. I loved when I could respond, "Busy!" to the question, "How are you?" My pace was a badge I showed off proudly, stealing time from family or sleep just to keep up. The kicker was that the more my influence increased, the more responsibility I was given. More responsibility meant more tasks and my personality went into overdrive to power through them; I thought that it was my only choice. "After all," I thought, "This is what successful people have to do."

This busy mind-set spilled over into my days "off"—there was never a day just dedicated to recalibrating—and then vacations. To get me to get away and make an attempt at relaxation, we purchased a pop-up camper. I am embarrassed to admit that, in the first couple of years of camping, I would drag a desktop computer (this was before the days of laptops) on vacation and justify that if I got up and worked for a few hours, I could then spend the rest of the day with the family. My wife stewed about this. She had every right to; I had no margins in my life.

The problem with my approach was that what seemed like productivity is really doing just enough to get by. What seems like accomplishing is really just surviving because that comet speed approach to getting it all done just means that people are not getting your best. Those who are closest to you get even less. There is little margin to delight, to enjoy or to take in the moment. I know. You just move on to the next thing. No margins!

> THERE IS A MARGIN FEW PEOPLE TALK ABOUT! THE MARGIN OF OUR TIME; THAT'S RIGHT, VERY RARELY DO WE GIVE ANY ATTENTION TO THE MARGINS OF OUR TIME.

The current economic status of most organizations and households has given a new perspective on the importance of margins. Barely a week goes by when a conversation doesn't include some reference to how all of us are managing the new reality of lower margins: we measure the margins, control the margins, manage the margins, hold people accountable to the margins, blah, blah, blah!

There is a margin few people talk about!

The margin of our time; that's right, very rarely do we give any attention to the margins of our time.

What our culture celebrates, either consciously or

subconsciously, is busy, jam-packed schedules. Calendars are full. We fall into bed exhausted, or, in some cases, it begins on the couch the first time we sit down for the evening. We wake up in the morning, dreading the appointments, the practices, and the commitments that await us. Our life is so full there is little margin. People tell me, "It's just crazy!" Brené Brown calls out the truth, "It takes courage to say yes to rest and play in a culture where exhaustion is seen as a status symbol." (*Dose of Daring*)

When I was in college and grad school, I had a different approach to managing margins. I liked them and I was great at making them. With every paper I wrote, and there were dozens, I became more skilled at making sure there were plenty of margins, both in my papers and in my life. I wasn't going to do more work than I had to do; I liked leaving space for me, even if what I did with that space now makes me shake my head with wonder. I wanted to make sure I got the maximum use out of margins each and every time.

Upon graduation, I bought the lie that margins were bad. Only lazy people had margins. Hard-working, driven, career-minded professionals filled their margins. And so I adapted by filling my margins. I prided myself on my ability to have no space in my calendar: the top, the bottom, and the sides were full. It became my way of measuring usefulness: my margins were as full as, if not fuller than, yours.

As I was learning to move from the transaction mind-set to the transformational mind-set, someone introduced me to the writing of Richard Swenson (*Restoring Margin to Overloaded Lives*). Subsequently, he has written other books on margins. He would have called my lifestyle at that time an "Overload Syndrome." I didn't know whether to be offended or complimented by his claim. Until I started studying his principles, that is. "Margin is the amount available beyond that which is needed. It is something held in reserves..." I was supposed to have something left?

I felt as if I were entering a twelve-step program for margin-less addicts. I had to work every step; the first step was admitting that I had a problem with the whole concept of having reserves in my life that would create emotional and relational health.

> HAVING MARGINS AFFORDS ME THE OPPORTUNITY TO LIVE WITH A CHILDLIKE SENSE OF WONDER.

After years of confronting my overloaded life head-on and working through the steps of recovery—yes, steps four and five were brutal, as I had to confess to my family what my marginless career life meant for them—I am learning the joy of having space. In fact, I'm learning that creating space is one of the best gifts I can give to myself and to others.

Don't get me wrong; there are moments when I look at my calendar and am tempted to think that my identity might have deeper meaning if only it were fuller. Then I take a deep breath and pause and remember that being overloaded is far from a badge of honor. Now, I leave spaces in my calendar. I even schedule space in my calendar. I anticipate good things that might fill the time. I am learning to see space as a gift for a conversation, a cup of coffee, or meditating. Having margins affords me the opportunity to live with a childlike sense of wonder. It sounds wonderful...now, I just need to practice it more.

Steps 1–5 of a Marginless Life

1. I admit that I am powerless over my life and that I live on a "busy autopilot": my schedule has become unmanageable, controlled by others or by own commitments so that my life is jammed full—whether during the work hours, the evening hours, or the weekends. I am driven to exhaustion and am regularly tired—overtired. I am not fully present to people or conversations. I live with an ache of never being fully satisfied. I am quickly on to the "next thing."

2. I believe that a power greater than me has to restore me to sanity and a life with rest, play, and recreation. Those closest to me have given up, because I continually make excuses for my radical behavior.

3. I decide to turn my will over to the care of God, as I understand him. Currently my will and my behavior are entirely out of balance. In fact, I tend to shame others less busy than me and to judge them, and I am annoyed by anybody that reminds me of being a slacker.

4. I take a moral inventory of my choices around being busy. I start with looking at my calendar for any margins or the lack thereof. I notice how I fill any extra space with something or someone. Then, I ask myself tough questions, "Why do I have to be busy? Why does my schedule have to be full? Why do I mindlessly check my phone? Why do I panic when I am away from my cell phone? Why does there always have to be noise? Why do I avoid silence?"

5. I admit the exact consequences of my decisions: being

tired, being exhausted, being imbalanced, making broken promises, having fractured relationships, having shallow conversations, and more.

Breathe and Pause

What would happen if you decided to manage the margins of your time?

What would it take for you to create more margins?

Friendship...is born at the moment when one man says to another, "What! You too? I thought that no one but myself..."
–C.S. LEWIS

There is nothing I would not do for those who are really my friends. I have no notion of loving people by halves, it's not my nature. –JANE AUSTIN

CHAPTER 19

Being a Friend

After a chapter on community, why have a chapter on friendship? Because stories of friendship shape WHO I am, WHAT I am up against, and HOW I will show up as a friend, giving and receive friendship.

According to *Clifton StrengthsFinder* I have the Talent Theme of Relator in my Top Five. The fundamental characteristic of the Relator theme is the way we find ways to identify with people. It doesn't mean that those without this Talent Theme do not. It's that Relators are innately wired to approach life, striving for some type of relational connection. Therefore, the only way relationships at any level work for us is that relationships must be genuine. Ripples may be a way to describe the way we view relationships.

The inner ring would consist of a tight-knit circle of people with whom we have a bond that is both close and personal. The next ring would consist of our friends with whom we click. The third ring would consist of people with whom we have connected, either personally or professionally. The fourth ring consists of all our acquaintances. We seem to know enough about people in that ring that, at any given point, we could connect with them.

Given this context, I propose that different types of communities fall into the third or fourth ring of relationships. Friendships fall into the inner or second ring. This is where authenticity leads to transparency and, in some cases intimacy.

This is not about labeling relationships. There is no forced ranking. I want people to see the beauty and complexity of relationships and not to approach them haphazardly. While it may seem that relationships just happen, they do not. They deserve our attention and certainly some intentionality.

We know that certain relationships last only for a time. You were close, maybe even friends. However, because of a move, a season of life, or a variety of other issues, you are now not close—that is, you are not friends any longer. It isn't that the friendship wasn't real or genuine. This is part of the rhythm of life.

Sometimes these friendships end badly. There is a riff, a broken bond of trust, or maybe stone-cold silence that would describe the way the friendship ended. Again, it doesn't negate what bond you once shared. This causes many people to be skeptical of having any close friends, moving forward. I have seen too many shut down their hearts so that they won't be hurt again and, in doing so, confess that they would rather be lonely than hurt. That is sad.

On the other hand, I have seen very close friends fall out of touch and then rekindle the friendship years, sometimes decades later. After tears, maybe even a confession of misunderstanding or betrayal, the friends reengage at an even more mature level.

I write about this because I have been a part of friendships that have not ended well. With a level of sadness, I confess there are times that I stiffed past friends with silence and others with harsh words. With a level of sorrow, I have also been on the receiving end of silence, harsh words, and betrayal. Those two emotions are chosen intentionally: sadness and sorrow. Sadness is about unhappiness or even regret, whereas as sorrow is about loss or misfortune, grieving. This is not semantics. If I am going to show up authentically, I need to be clear about my emotions. Sometimes, friendships lead me to respond with sadness; at other times, they lead me to respond with sorrow. When I can accept that this is a part of being genuinely connected as a friend, I can let go of my expectations and experience love—forgiveness, joy, gratitude, and more—in my friendships. This is the mark of transformational person.

I have friends in both the inner and second ring of my life. In every case, we have had conversations about our friendship, what it means, what are healthy boundaries, and what are fair expectations, given whatever season of life each of us may be in or where we live. When I think about friendship, I find that the following behaviors are practiced regularly. Yes, they come naturally in most cases, and if not, our friendships have enough space for one of us to ask for it by saying, "This is what I need!" One of the most vulnerable things to do.

The Hallmark of Friends:

- **We are reciprocal.** There will be times when one of us is up and the other down, and vice versa. Friendship isn't a one-way street when it comes to building each other up, helping each other out, sorting through issues, and more. When it's a one-way street, that would be called ministry (Merriam Webster's Dictionary)—"attend to the needs of"—that is not being a friend.

- **We are bonded by core values.** I did not have a category like this until several years ago, when I realized the value and power of core values. As I listened to stories of broken friendships and what bonded new ones, the stories were always around core values. If some friends don't align with your core values, it just means that they are driven by something different than you, and it will be a challenge to develop a tight bond with them. Core value misalignment will surface regularly, and it will cause you to wonder why some people that you like don't seem to jell. They may remain acquaintances, but close friendships with them cannot be developed.

- **We accept each other's strengths and weaknesses.** There are two important principles in this hallmark. The first is acceptance. This doesn't mean that I necessarily like their strengths or weaknesses; but it does mean that I do more than tolerate them. The action is to accept, receive, consent, and affirm. And it is an action – to see what friends bring to the table and to value them for it. Second, acceptance is about creating space. Creating space for friends to flourish in their strengths by seeking their help or insight and creating space for their weakness by giving them room to struggle or get frustrated. Frustrated with their weaknesses and whatever comes with that. The bow that ties acceptance and space together is grace. It's grace that doesn't judge. It's grace that gives space. It's grace that pulls them up. It's grace that spurs them on.

- **We trust each other.** Trust is a loaded word. When I ask people what they mean by trust, I usually get a blank stare along with, "You know...uh...trust...uh!" Exactly which is why Chris and I at Nexecute define trust as "a decision to let go based on a belief that the intention and the ability of the other is good." This universal definition applies in every relationship. Out of the gate, if we are in relationship, I must make the first move of trust: to let go. Of what I let go depends on our relationship. It starts with letting go of control, because control is a relationship killer. People ask, "Do I have to trust blindly?" Not at all.

> A DECISION TO LET GO BASED ON A BELIEF THAT THE INTENTION AND THE ABILITY OF THE OTHER IS GOOD.

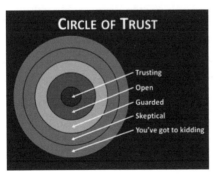

CIRCLE OF TRUST

- Trusting
- Open
- Guarded
- Skeptical
- You've got to kidding

In the movie *Meet the Parents,* Robert De Niro

plays the character of Jack Byrnes and introduces his son-in-law to the Circle of Trust. In his world, one is either "in" or "out" of the Circle of Trust, albeit by his or her choice.

I find people have certain natural inclinations to the levels of trust they offer. The diagram shows the range. I have met people who identify with each ring of the circle. Again, that is their natural bent, ranging from "trusting" to "you've got to be kidding." It's important you know your own starting point of trust.

Where you start impacts the next step: "based on a belief." Let's be honest: you never know how much you can trust someone, so you make a judgment call based upon a belief, maybe a gut feeling. Again, this isn't done blindly. It is based on one of two key factors: intent and ability. If you believe someone's intent is good, you can start with a green light of trust. If you have some doubt, it's a yellow light, and you proceed with caution. Once you fully trust someone's intent, it's a green light.

Once intent is determined, now you can proceed to ability. You may completely trust some people's intent but are not sure about their abilities. At this point, the conversation is about what knowledge or skill is needed for you to trust them. The more they learn, the more you trust their abilities.

You may think this process of trust is too complicated or at least too cumbersome. I would disagree. If you do this type of work on the front end of any relationship and then practice it throughout the relationship, you establish clear boundaries. Life will be so much easier. Believe me. I know what happens without this type of clarity.

Once trust is established, it shows up in three distinct ways. I am inspired by what is known as the "Love Chapter" in the Bible (1 Corinthians 13):

Love protects. It's good to be protected, to feel safe. In friendship, you get space to admire and maybe even emulate a friend's good qualities or special skills. There will be times when, out of your humanity, you will offer the opposite of protection. So what do you do? You will be tempted to blame, to be a victim, or to make your friends pay. Choosing love would mean being humble and would, together with love, protect your friendship, shielding instead of shaming.

Love hopes. It's reassuring to know that you have friends you can expect good things from and who will push through fear with you. There will be times when out of your humanity will come a fear that will squelch each other's hope. You will be tempted to pull away from your friends, but love hopes. So what do you do? Choosing love is choosing to humble yourself enough to move toward those friendships. To genuinely seek out the truth, live in your natural talents, and to know that you can bring out the best in them as they do in you.

Love perseveres. It's comforting to know that you have friends who are loyal; enduring challenges and celebrating joys. And there will be times when, out of your humanity, you will grow impatient with your friends and become exasperated with them. So what do you do? You will be tempted to be cynical and to think that they don't understand you, maybe feeling alone. Odd? But it happens. Choosing love would mean being humble enough to be truly vulnerable with them, to speak the truth in love to them, and to forgive them.

One of my friends, Matt Emhoff, is young enough to be

my son and wise enough to be my mentor. Actually, I was his mentor for a season. It wasn't long before it was clear to both of us that, for many reasons, we were best served if we became friends. Our relationship was fast becoming reciprocal, and our core values were becoming aligned. The more we learned about each other's strengths, the more we were drawn to learn more about them and about each other. This began the deep dive into all the layers of trust.

I was watching Matt come into his own. For lack of a better analogy, Matt was finding his voice. He grew up in a home where keeping rules were of high importance, so he spent little time thinking about who he was outside of the compliance expected. For Matt to find his voice, it meant exploring the depths of who he was inside this role and outside of it; he had to figure out how he showed up in the world. We shared hours of conversation, often over a good cigar. It was clear to many others and me that Matt was wise beyond his years and that he had a strong commitment to his transformation.

> WE ARE MEANT TO SHINE, AND WHEN WE SHINE, PEOPLE EXPERIENCE THE WEIGHTINESS OF OUR LIFE.

He grew in confidence exponentially, and people responded to the depth of his thinking and his penetrating questions. I don't recall how the conversation started, but I remember saying to Matt, "You have so much to offer, and I don't want you to hold anything back when you are with me. Bring it on; I am not put off by your power!" It was as if a dam had burst, and each time I was with Matt, he showed up with his power: the depth of his character and the ideas of an elder statesman. He didn't have the hubris I had when I was his age. Matt had a humble confidence.

It may seem odd to say to some people that we can handle their power. What does that mean? I know what it means to feel the shame of inadequacy. I have also lived with the fear of not being able to fully show up as myself, withholding my power and living small. We are meant to shine, and when we shine, people experience the weightiness of our life—the glory that is within us. Marianne Williamson (*A Return to Love*) offers the unique perspective,

> Our deepest fear is not that we are inadequate. Our deepest fear is that we are powerful beyond measure. It is our light, not our darkness, that most frightens us. We ask ourselves, "Who am I to be brilliant, gorgeous, talented, fabulous?" Actually, who are you not to be? You are a child of God. Your playing small does not serve the world. There is nothing enlightened about shrinking so that other people won't feel insecure around you. We are all meant to shine, as children do. We were born to make manifest the glory of God that is within us. It's not just in some of us; it's in everyone. And as we let our own light shine, we unconsciously give other people permission to do the same. As we are liberated from our own fear, our presence automatically liberates others.

It took me a lifetime to believe that I was born to manifest the goodness within me. The more I embrace it, the more I give people permission to do the same. True friendship means that we don't have to "play small" with each other. Rather, we can liberate each other when we live out of the weightiness of our life. I now have these deep, heart-level conversations with my closest friends.

It was months later when Matt walked into my home office and asked if we could talk. People who are close to Matt know that when he has that steely determination in his eyes and the tone of voice that says, "We about to go deep!" that it's going to be challenging—good but challenging. It was. Matt knew me well enough to ask the hard questions. He knew my strengths well enough to notice that I was not leaning into them in a certain circumstance. He watched me acquiesce when I usually am in the mix. Because he knew me well, he could ask the deeper question, "What's that all about?" We talked. Matt listened. I got vulnerable. Matt was compassionate. We came out of it with a stronger bond and better people for it. We were liberated.

Henry Ford once said, "My best friend is the one who brings out the best in me." My close friends bring out the best in me. They tell me I bring out the best in them. I am so grateful.

Breathe and Pause

Who are people that you would consider friends that fall into your inner relational rings?

What do you experience with your friends? How can you bring each other your power?

How do your friendships align with the Hallmarks of Friendship?

*You cannot tailor-make the situations in life, but you can
tailor-make the attitudes to fit those situations.* –Zig Ziglar

Man often becomes what he believes himself to be.
–Mahatma Gandhi

CHAPTER 20

My Resolve

I am intrigued by the word manifesto—manifestō "a public
declaration of policy and aims." The etymology is Latin, *infes-
tus*, something that is easy to perceive or recognize.

Over millennia, it seems that people like to make a declaration but often do not link their behavior to it. This leaves an
incongruency.

As I move into the last third of my life, I want to be con-
gruent, more often having my behaviors match more closely
with what I believe. To do so does not come about by wishing
it were so. Transformation doesn't just happen. It takes effort.
The man who taught me so much about grace also taught
me about the important role of effort. They are not mutually
exclusive. Rather, they are the two essential components of
a transformational life. Dallas Willard wrote, "Grace is not

opposed to effort, it is opposed to earning. Earning is an attitude. Effort is an action" (*The Great Omission*).

My story is one of effort: from transactional effort driven by EGO to transformational effort that transcends EGO. The latter is motivated by grace. What is your story, your motivation, your manifesto?

Below is my manifesto. It's more than a declaration; it's my resolve. These statements define what it means for me to relax in grace, combined with the effort it takes to live mindfully, thereby letting the results be what they are. It's the basis of being a transformational person.

How do you want to show up, making transactions or living in a transformational way? The choice is yours. Let me know what you resolve to do.

I resolve to

- Courageously live my story: core values, purpose, and mission

- Live as a transformational person

- Leave a meaningful legacy

- Be an influence for good and engage others in pursuing it

- Choose character over reputation

- Make the choice of having a positive attitude

- Have a vision for my future

- Clarify my intentions

- Authentically invest in relationships

- Lean into the role of process in all areas of my life and take responsibility for my life: physically, intellectually, relationally, emotionally, and spiritually

- Accept that I am accountable for my responses to life
- Recognize that everyone else is a free agent with the right to choose
- Enjoy the power of friendship: bringing my power and accepting my friends' power
- Accept the importance of conflict resolution and ruthlessly practice it
- Understand my "Adversity Quotient" in overcoming obstacles and setbacks
- Be a person of grace: loving God and loving others as I love myself

Love is the strongest force in the universe. Gravity may hold planets in orbit and nuclear force may hold the atom together but only love has the power to transform persons. Only love can renew trust after it has been shattered. Only love can inspire acts of genuine self-sacrifice. And only love can free us from the tyrannizing effects of fear.

DAVID G. BENNER – *Surrender to Love*

To see what people are saying about the book
and to join the conversation go to
www.thechoicetoshowup.com

Letter to a College Student

My Young Friend,

You've made it through your teenage years. That is a feat!

You've decided on a career as an executive. That took guts!

What you do next will take courage.

By that, I don't mean being brave or trying to accomplish something heroic. There are too many war stories of executives, young and old alike, who have left a wake of destruction in their professional and personal careers by trying to be or to do something in the name of "making an impact" or being noticed.

What I mean by courage harkens back to the origin of the word from Latin: COURAGE [cor]— heart—"to speak one's mind by telling all one's heart." Dr Brené Brown reiterates that courage is the choice "to tell the story of who you are with your whole heart." The best gift you will give to yourself and others is to courageously live from your heart—your whole heart.

I know that college was about what you could produce from your mind. I know that, in your career, you will be measured by the power of your mind. I am not negating the role of your brain. What I am saying is that you must make the choice to live, to work, and to relate to others from your whole heart. Notice the differentiator. It's not just from your heart, because your heart, my heart, is damaged, broken, and frail. Rather, as Dr. Brown states, it's living from your whole heart. "Wholehearted living is about engaging in our lives from a place of worthiness. It means cultivating the courage, compassion, and connection to wake up in the morning and think, no matter what gets done and how much is left undone, I am enough."

That may seem painfully obvious, at best, or, at worst, trite. But most people I meet in business and in life try to prove they are enough or they have what it takes. That is the drive you will encounter in the business world, whether it's in profit or nonprofit. I know because I was one of those people. They (I) will mask that they have it all together. They (I) develop elaborate mechanisms to pose so that you see someone who is put together. They (I) will hope you don't ever find out that they are human, frail, or broken. They (I) will avoid vulnerability and, therefore, make it difficult to trust them [me].

We live that way, because we don't know our story. That means that we don't know the truth of WHO we are, WHERE we came from, and WHAT we are up against.

I know that I didn't have the courage or the tenacity to look deep within. I focused on the 10 percent of the iceberg that was above the waterline, and I avoided the 90 percent of what is in the depths of my being. I just kept striving, hoping that, with each accomplishment, it would be enough to show people that I was good. How empty that hope was!

I remember reading these words from Dee Hock, "The first and paramount responsibility of anyone who purports to manage (or lead) is to manage self…It is a complex unending incredibly difficult, oft-shunned task. Without management of self, no one is fit for authority no matter how much they acquire, for the more authority they acquire the more dangerous they become" (*Chaordic Leadership*).

As a young person (husband, father, friend, leader), I had no idea about how to approach self-management. Now, as someone at this stage of my life who spends time coaching and mentoring others, I confidently share with you that your courageous journey to self-awareness and self-management is the best gift you will give yourself and others.

I didn't do that for two decades. I made decisions that were driven by my EGO and my self-protection. I know what it means to try to get from other people what they cannot give you: validation. I know the impact of spending a lifetime of motivating people to see things my way and of not having the insight to know that they saw through me and the selfishness of my motivations. I know what it's like to be so wounded and not to have the courage to face it and, by not facing it, inflicting my woundedness on others, mostly subconsciously. I know what it means to have to come to "the end of my rope," and I know that my only choice was to surrender and to learn to change from the inside out.

I had to learn about being a transformational person so that I could eventually be a transformational leader. Transformational leadership is based on two fundamental principles: self-awareness and self-management. If you accept that change happens from the inside out, you will ruthlessly choose to pay attention to your interior world, and by doing so, it will impact your exterior world.

You will approach work differently. You will embrace change: accept change, identify what needs to change, create a vision for change, and inspire change throughout the organization, thereby attracting people to sacrifice perceived self-interest for a genuinely appealing collective purpose. Why? Because you do.

I am a living testimony that, with focused, intentional effort and the guidance of those who love me, you can live wholeheartedly. I am learning to live honestly, authentically, and with inner freedom. I know what it means to serve others out of a settled purpose and clear values. I know what it's means to be transformative.

Frankly, most leaders would rather just work in the business than developing their own skills. The speed of business demands it, and revenue dictates it. Therefore, it takes a conscious decision to dedicate time and energy to personal development and to take your own development as seriously as the top-line and bottom-line numbers in the business.

There is so much more to share. You have a lifetime to learn about transformation. May I encourage you to unpack your story. Then read, listen to podcasts, journal, learn how to recreate well, create margins in your schedule, self-reflect, and more. Find other leaders with whom you can develop authentic relationships. Do whatever you can to find mentors who have traveled the path before. Schedule time with them. Furthermore, hire a coach to provide a safe space to be vulnerable, who will ask you the right questions, challenge your misperceptions, and encourage you to be audacious in both your personal and professional life.

Enjoy the journey and be courageous!

Ten Things I Learned about Transformation

(Summarized in my words)

1. You won't change until the pain on the outside matches the pain on the inside.

2. If you want to change your exterior world, you must deal with your interior world.

3. Begin to embrace the truth that solitude is the furnace of transformation.

4. We will be hurt ourselves, and we will hurt others, until we face what's below the waterline of our iceberg.

5. There is a great difference between trying harder and training.

6. Transformation doesn't happen by accident.

7. Transformation happens best in a community with people you trust.

8. A wound that we ignore or do not weep over cannot be healed.

9. Strength is found in surrender.

10. Read the story of your life, and take it seriously.

ABOUT THE AUTHOR

Mark took a circuitous path to his current role as cofounder of Nexecute, LLC, where he and his partner, Chris Elias, advise leaders and executives, provide structure and processes, and build transformational teams that optimize results.

Believing people can make a unique contribution to our world, Mark invites people to transform from the inside out and supports them in reaching their fullest potential. A Master's of Divinity provides a solid foundation for him as an accomplished teacher, writing curricula and teaching transformational principles. This experience has given Mark depth and credibility in creating environments, where he invites individuals to change their lives in coaching sessions, as well as inspiring and challenging groups of people in creative learning sessions for educators, corporate workgroups, business owners, students, and nonprofit leaders.

His first position after seminary afforded him the opportunity to think outside the box in developing curricula, from children to adults, with the goal of creating experiential learning environments. These early years of experimenting with educational applications were foundational in crystallizing his desire to have people "actually learn." They also embodied his belief that challenging people to look inside and think differently just might be the seedbed of transformation.

He served in a variety of congregations, inspiring people as an innovative leader and a cultural change agent.

Mark's belief in transformation isn't just theoretical. In

1994, his personal and professional lives were reset after a bout with thyroid cancer, surgery, radiation treatment, losing a job, and a subsequent cross-country move that upended his family. Through it all, he learned that the greatest gift he could give others was a life that was grounded with a clarity of purpose and values. It was during this time that he was introduced to the principles of Transformational Leadership and Actual Change Theory; living from solid principles and serving others was the way of greatest influence.

In 2004, he resigned from ministerial life and focused on how he could impact organizational health. He spent five years as the general manager of a conference center, where his mandate was to build a cohesive leadership team and a healthy culture. This would springboard Mark into his current passion for helping people transform and into his career as a trusted advisor.

Mark and his high school sweet-heart Debbie celebrate forty years of marriage and live in southeast Michigan. They truly enjoy their family: Anne, Katie & husband Dan, Nathan & wife Angela, and, of course, their grandchildren, Abigail, Graham, and Logan.